*The Ice at the
End of the World*

The Ice at the End of the World

Robert Siegel

HarperSanFrancisco
A Division of HarperCollins*Publishers*

Acknowledgments: The verse fragments quoted on pages 9, 20, 94, and 219 are taken, with slight alteration, from Blake's "The Tyger," Tennyson's "The Kracken," Wordsworth's "The World Is Too Much with Us," and Coleridge's *The Rime of the Ancient Mariner.*

FIRST EDITION

Library of Congress Cataloging-in-Publication Data
Siegel, Robert, 1939-
    The ice at the end of the world / Robert Siegel.
      p. cm.
    ISBN 0-06-250805-9 (cloth)
    ISBN 0-06-250806-7 (paper)
    1. Whales—Fiction.   I. Title.
PS3569.I382I2   1994
813'.54—dc20   93-41091
                                           CIP

---

99 00 01 02 03 ❖ RRD(H)   10 9 8 7 6 5 4 3

For
Lenaye,
Lucy,
and
Christine

A Key to Pronouncing the Whale Names

The initial H is aspirated (pronounced in a breathy manner).

Aleea:	A-LEE'A
Bala:	BA'LA
Hralekana:	hRA-LA-KA'NA
Hreelëa:	hREE-LEE'A
Hrekka:	hREK'KA
Hrēta:	hREE'TA
Hrobo:	hRO'BO
Hrūna:	hROO'NA
Hrunta:	hRUN'TA
Hvala:	hVA'LA
Kaleea:	KA-LEE'A
Lewtë:	LOO'TA
Lūvah:	LOO'vah

A Note to the Reader

When toward the end of White Whale, *a young marine biologist tries to prevent a nuclear test in the ocean by sailing his ship into the testing zone, the white Humpback whale Hralekana follows him and discovers a limpet mine saboteurs have attached to the ship's hull. In an attempt to save Mark and the ship, Hralekana carries the mine into the Deep and suffers a serious wound. The wounded whale is carried by his grieving pod to an underwater cave, where he descends alone.* The Ice at the End of the World *begins with Hralekana narrating the story just after he enters the cave.*

And now there came both mist and snow,
And it grew wondrous cold:
And ice, mast-high, came floating by,
As green as emerald.

    — *The Rime of the Ancient Mariner*

The bones cry for the blood of the white whale,

.   .   .   .

Where the morning stars sing out together
And thunder shakes the white surf. . . .

   .   .   .   . Hide,

Our steel, Jonas Messias, in Thy side.

    — *The Quaker Graveyard in Nantucket*

Chapter One

The word repeated itself over and over while I lay there in the cave, each repetition rising toward the surface like a bubble, each one louder than the last. The word uttered itself, moving through me in a wave, each time taking more of the weariness and pain and bringing me new strength and clarity of mind. The rocks around me glowed with a dim phosphorescence, reminding me of other days I had spent in this undersea cavern. In their light I faced the dark opening through which my word resonated, I knew, to those on the surface.

Again I spoke it, and again. Each time I felt electrified, as when the water is struck in a thunderstorm by Ohobo's flashing harpoon. My whole body, from my flippers to the tips of my flukes, quivered at the word. The wound in my belly gave off the merest thread of blood and the pain there grew numb. My light-headedness from loss of blood diminished, receding like a beach as the tide comes in, wave after wave.

Lying there, I thought about the last time I was in this under-sea cavern and about all that had happened since. I relived knocking the limpet mine from the hide of the *Rainbow Whale* and carrying it to the Deep, where it exploded, wounding me. But it had not hurt the yellow ship or my friend Mark. Even as I lay there, Mark and the crew were sailing to confront the warships, the gray fleet that carried another man-made device to blow up an island and poison the ocean. By now they must have caught up with the fleet, and I worried for their lives.

I recalled my last sight of the ship and Mark, his small figure waving from the rail.

Afterward, bleeding from my side and supported by Aleea, my mate, my father Hrūna, and others of the pod, I swam to the waters above Hralekana's cavern. Leaving my friends on top, with my last strength I plunged down to it.

My thoughts turned again to those waiting above who had carried me to this place, grieving. I knew they heard me repeat the word. I also knew that in their joy that I was still alive, they wanted to dive down to me—Aleea and my mother Lewtë, especially. I knew it took all their willpower to follow my last request—that, whatever happened, they not dive down.

While the mists fled from the rising sun, each of them (as they told me later) had ached to dive. But they held back while my word rose from the depths, staring at one another in stunned surprise, too glad for speech.

They listened a long time and then Hrūna gave a brief command: All except Aleea, Lewtë, and himself would carry the news to the rest of the pod, now on its yearly journey to the Ice at the End of the World. At Hrūna's word, they sped away into the dissolving mist. The three who remained lay in a circle around the spot where I dove and listened. As my word came louder and stronger, their eyes brightened. They later said it was like listening to the voice of the earth itself resounding from the center.

Later, lying in the cave, I heard the faint strains of their response—the voice of Aleea soon joined by Lewtë. Aleea said that the song burst from her spontaneously; she later named it the Song of Waiting:

> *Fresh blows the wind from the dawn's gold mouth*
> *Over the bright and blue green sea,*

Driving the heavy fog from my heart.
How the light leaps from wave to wave!
When will my love return to me?

Their silvery voices twined and echoed, winding down through the opening to the cave like some light and invisible kelp. Hearing them, I sang my word louder, its echo reverberating against the walls of the cave and expanding through that cold sea for any and all to hear.

How I wanted to leave the cave and rise up to them! But I knew what I had to do in the cave was just beginning. I didn't know what that was, though obviously I was healing. I had a strong sense that I was waiting for something, and what that something was would become clearer as I repeated the word over and over. I lay there, saying the word and trying not to think of anything else.

I don't know whether I fell asleep or not, but it seemed like hours later that I noticed the glowing walls of the cave growing dimmer and the water colder. I tried to move but felt sluggish. The light faded to the barest glimmer, and the cold pierced me like an icicle. My flippers and flukes stiffened.

Then all was darkness.

Above, as they told me later, they heard my voice fade and the word come slower and slower. Finally it stopped altogether. There was only silence. For them it was the darkest moment of all. The miraculous surprise earlier—my voice rising to them, rekindling hope—now seemed a cruel joke. They lay there in a stupor of grief. None could speak or look at the others. As if to mark the fading hope of dawn, clouds gathered and rain fell in a drizzle. The three lay mute, listening for the slightest sound.

I must have lapsed into unconsciousness for a while. Then in the blackness and cold, I suddenly came to, and the drowsiness lifted. It was as if someone had spoken and wakened me. My mind was reduced to a point, sharp and alert, but my physical strength was gone. I couldn't feel my flippers or flukes.

Yet while I lay there, strength returned. All remained dark, but I felt a new power move into my belly and flukes. Suddenly, without thinking about it, I swam out of the cave. Instinctively I moved through the opening: it was as if something were calling me.

Once outside, I plunged farther down into the abyss of that cold sea. I went down, it seemed, forever. The water was colder than before and gripped me like ice. Now and then a whisper just beyond the threshold of hearing came from below. I sped down into the darkness.

Dark as the water was, a deeper dark opened below me. I came to the entrance of a cave or tunnel in the bottom and, without hesitating, swam into it. The walls of the tunnel closed in around me, and a faint electrical whisper took shape in the water.

"*Hraleh. . .*"—it brushed by my ear like a silken fin—"*. . . kana.*" My heart skipped a beat, for I thought I recognized that voice.

The farther down I swam, the louder it sounded.

"*Hralekana,*" At last it came clearly, and I paused—at a loss—for I did know that voice, a voice that had spoken to me twice before. Where I stopped, the walls of the tunnel widened into a vastness, an ocean under the earth.

The cold, if anything, was more intense and pierced me like a harpoon.

"I am here," I said in a small voice. The underearth ocean was so large that not the faintest echo of my words came back.

In the distance I saw a flash, then darkness. The flash reappeared as a point of intense white light, moving toward me. Soon it took a familiar shape, a great way off, no bigger than a star in the night sky. Closer and closer it came, swelling until it dwarfed and blinded me. I was a krill that could float between two of its baleen. Behind it shone—though I didn't understand how in this underearth ocean—all the stars of the heavens.

The mouth spread wide in the smile that, as one of our ancestors sang, kindled the universe. It spoke my name, *Hralekana-kolua*, in a musical phrase that seemed to go on forever.

"My son," the Whale of Light spoke, "you have done *well*." And, as he said it, the word rang out from the stars behind him.

Embarrassed, I looked down. And the voice called out, "Rejoice!" The stars swelled in chorus, and their lights flashed and turned while they sang high and low.

At last, the look upon the ineffable Face turned grave, filled with pity while he spoke: "To do what I ask next, you must understand matters that are hidden—about the foundation of all things and how they have fared even from the beginning to the present."

Then, I know not how, the Whale of Light vanished, and I was left looking at the stars. In a moment, his voice came from behind me.

"Behold," he said, "the Beginning." At that word, the stars disappeared and before me lay darkness absolute. Then the Whale of Light sang, and as he sang, the words took shape before my eyes. Each word sprang up as the thing named, far beyond my power to describe. The musical language was living and vibrant and grew into the very things themselves. The words in which I recall this fade before the reality.

First, as I said, I saw the absolute darkness of the Void. Suddenly in the black I heard a deep outrushing of breath and felt a great wind, the force of which nearly swept me away.

Then I heard a word, a long, yearning cry, and in the darkness appeared a brilliant pinpoint of light and a white flash that filled my whole field of vision, nearly blinding me.

When the flash cleared, I saw wheeling from the center stars and galaxies and red and purple nebulae. The center flashed and pulsed as the stars came forth, spreading out before me. With a shock, I realized I was looking straight down into the blowhole of the Whale of Light from which all streamed toward me.

In awe and terror I turned aside, and when I looked again, my point of view had changed, for I saw now from the side the most beautiful spout ever, a fountain rising high into the endless abyss. The brilliant stars each had the shape of a whale with flippers and flukes spread out in rays of light. These were the Stars of the Morning. When all were in place, they sang, and their voices rang in chorus to the Voice singing the Song of Creation:

> *In the wide abyss the word is uttered,*
> *Day springs forth and darkness flees.*
> *One breath breathes all: each bright eye opens*
> *And the stars spin in galaxies.*

While they sang, their rays pierced the darkness like harpoons of light. The spears blazed forth, and the stars faded in a deep blue sky. Beneath it, silver waters stretched forever. The stars, each in its splendor, came down one at a time and plunged into the waters, rolling and breaching. Wherever one dived, shoals of fish and other creatures sprang forth from its light and fled into the Deep. Wherever one leaped out of the water, land rose under it, turning green as plants climbed to the music and festooned it with living vegetation.

It was indeed the Beginning, as one of our ancient singers sang,

When the stars threw down their spears
And watered heaven with their tears.

The stars continued to sing the song of Creation, swimming to and fro upon the waters. The tide rose and fell to the rhythm of their singing and the Red Bull of the Sun leaped to it, rising over the sky and plunging into the burning seas of the west. The White Cow of the Moon followed him in the darkness, scattering her milk over the waves and pulling the seas toward her, the ocean's belly rising round as her own.

The harmony was ravishing, except from one star whose luster had faded, from whom no splendor shone. I saw that this star's thoughts were inward and dark, for they clouded his bright, translucent being. Wherever this dark star dove under the waters or breached above new land rising, something came forth that was amiss. And no music came from this star, just the harsh wail of the wind over cliffs of stone and the thunder and crash of rock against rock in the heated bowels of the earth and the groan of cold ice grinding at the End of the World.

With these, the vision faded and in the dark the Voice sang, and his words came sad and low:

"As the Sons of the Morning swam forth upon the word to shape the waters, the earth, and the heavens, so went forth the nameless one to undo their work, creating for every something a nothing, a shadow for every light. He turned the stone cold and selfish in its weight and made the red lava angry till it seethed and hissed beneath it.

"Ever from that day have order and disorder been at war; creation has trembled over, even as it mastered, the chaos that resists the light. For in each thing is that which resists, as well as that which yearns for, what it is meant to become. The whole creation grumbles and struggles together waiting to put on the glory of the stars of the morning."

And then, the stars were silent and faded, and out of darkness came a thin, dry whisper, the Shadow's Song:

> There under each thing, the shadow swells thinly,
> Under each stone, the stark absence of light,
> The nothing from which all things come willy nilly
> And to which they return in the null of night.

The stars came back, and the Voice continued: "And so the light burns bright for a while, then the dark snuffs it, just as the Red Bull of the Sun is quenched by the waves each evening. But the light returns, just as the Red Bull breaches bright again in the morning. So the shadow falls, like nightshade, but even in the night the White Cow of the Moon reflects the light of the Red Bull, and the stars shine forth, so that hope is given to humans and whales, and a beautiful thing is made of the dark."

While he sang this, his voice lost its mournful tone and the dissonance of the starry chorus resolved into a deep note of harmony.

"And so," he continued, "will it ever be—the evil seeming to triumph and the good altering and overcoming it, age after age, as the waves wear away and add to the shore, until in the fullness of time one comes forth to pierce with light the very heart of the shadow and bring all things to completion.

"But the shadow will not give over without a struggle, and its latter upheavals may be greater than its former." The starry chorus crowded together, blazing while they sang:

> When night squeezes all in its squidlike coils,
> When hope has vanished and the heart is hollow,
> When evil like oil has oozed over ocean,
> In the darkness the dear one shall be delivered,
> And light shine forth from the flukes of the morning.

Once again the Whale of Light swam up to me, and his baleen shone so bright that I turned my head aside. He spoke words into my ear—not all of which I may repeat—and I knew why he had shown me the vision of the beginning of things and what he now asked me to do.

Chapter Two

When I opened my eyes again, I was in the sea tunnel, surrounded by total darkness. But I wasn't alone. I felt a presence with me, and the words of what I must do rang clearly in my head. Yet the blood flowed from my wound again, and more heavily, though I did not feel weak. I swam along the tunnel, the echoes giving it shape in the blackness. At times it opened out into wide underground seas and then narrowed again in places until there was barely room to pass.

I have no sense of how long this underearth journey lasted. It might have been hours, or days. The passage of time was not important to me now, after my encounter with the Whale of Light. At some point I became aware of a slight change in the deadly cold waters; there was a hint of warmth. Shortly after that I noticed something just at the threshold of hearing—a whisper, but not quite. The whisper came with a slight shift in the current. At times the current carried me forward, and at others resisted me, as if it were alternately flowing both ways in the tunnel. At last the whisper became audible.

It was a strange sound, a susurrus, as of water sucked through a giant set of gills or mouth or other aperture. I had never heard its like on so large a scale, and a shiver moved down my spine.

As the water gradually warmed, the darkness grew a shade lighter. In the distance I saw a faint glow; it was the end of the tunnel, still far off. The water continued to whisper, back and forth, and now it formed unclear words in a singsong pattern. The half-words made me uneasy.

At last the end of the tunnel gaped before me. The water there shone a pale, flickering gray. I swam ahead and in a moment was out of it.

I stopped. What lay before me nearly sucked the last air from me. For a moment my eyes wouldn't focus and my ears rang. I couldn't think to flee back into the shelter, such as it was, of the tunnel mouth. I floated there, my jaws open, my flippers useless at my sides.

It was monstrous. What lay before me was a vague, dim whiteness, shifting and flickering over miles, flitting and shuddering, coiling and uncoiling. Strange how in the moments of greatest fear, small, irrelevant details of a scene burn into one's memory. What I recall seeing in that shifting light—even before I understood what I saw—are the creatures that swam in a wide circle around it. There were the strange illuminated fish I had met before, moving in their own ghostly radiance. There were batfish and other fish with no eyes, including perfectly white blind shrimp, tubeworms waving like a forest of kelp, and hagfish spiraling up out of the sand to swallow the unwary.

From cracks in the cliffs surrounding this vast pit, the steam of white and black smokers escaped the scalding bowels of the earth. There was no hint of flame, no fiery cracks of magma or lava. Everything shone white and gray and black; the steam rose in clouds into the dark ocean piled miles above us.

While I tried to make sense of all this, I saw what appeared to be acres of pale, spotted flesh undulating, stretching for miles. Long peninsulas of it moved and shuddered, and in the distance rose to a central peak of flesh, like the dome of a mountain. The fleshy peninsulas extended and then coiled in upon themselves, much as low headlands taper into the ocean at ebb tide and shrink back at flood. The flesh rose to a quivering mountain, and there I saw the source of the ghastly light.

Two pale eyes, each much longer and wider than I, flashed out over the undulant soft flesh. The eyes shone bright, then clouded over as if the creature to whom they belonged was lost in some miasmal swamp of thought. I could discern no other features of a face, yet the monstrous shape looked somehow familiar.

Suddenly rushing toward me, uncoiling, rolled one of the monstrous headlands of flesh. I watched, mesmerized, before shaking myself awake and dodging as it cracked past me fast as a whip. I ducked back into the tunnel.

As it passed, I noticed round disks as large as manta rays on its underside, and suddenly I knew why I'd felt uneasy from the moment I'd discerned the whisper in the tunnel. The disks were monstrous versions of the suction cups on the tentacles of the giant squid that had seized me as a calf and from which Hrūna had rescued both Aleea and me.

My flesh recalled the strangling grip, and everything in me wanted to flee back up the tunnel. This, too, was a squid—but at that the comparison paled. For the earlier squid, which seemed so large at the time, filling the belly of the battleship, was to this as a herring is to a Blue whale, as a krill is to the icebergs it floats among.

This one was, unmistakably, the *Kraken,* of dreadful legend. At last the whisper grew clear, breathed with the current from that vast undulating hulk.

"*Hra . . . le . . . ka . . . na,*" the monster exhaled in a lurid, famished, and infinitely weary tone. "*Come. . . !*"

It took all my courage just to look out the mouth of the tunnel. What I saw nearly drove me back up it. For the eyes on that mountain of a head, pale and clouded a moment earlier, now blazed a cold bone-white, shining like fire from the lighthouses of men. They had no pupils and moved over the face of the cliff like twin searchlights looking for me.

The huge tentacle that I had barely escaped twitched back and forth, a hundred fathoms at a time, groping and sucking at the face of the cliff, pulling chunks of rock from it that crashed to the ocean floor. The Deep thundered and shook. Back and forth it felt and once even covered the mouth of the tunnel. Alarmed, I swam far up it, fearing the tip would enter.

Apparently it never sensed the opening, for it suddenly curled back toward the body of the Kraken and the eyes lost their luster as if the monster had lost interest. The light from them now only fitfully illuminated the pit, surrounded on all sides by cliffs stretching up into the darkness. The far side was an immense distance away. The creature appeared to forget my presence and sink back into itself.

This time I lurked just inside the mouth of the cave, looking out over the whole pit before exposing myself again to those pale eyes.

I knew from stories and legends whispered to me as a calf, as well as from what the Whale of Light had told me, who the Kraken was. Stretching over miles, here at the very bottom of the world, its sickly white a parody of the radiance of the Whale of Light himself, it lay, feeding on the carrion of the sea—and on whatever was unlucky enough to come down to it alive. Its spotted flesh evermoving and restless, its countless tentacles coiled and uncoiled like a nest of gigantic snakes, stretching like points of land from the continent of its bulk, curling and waving back and forth, hungry for whatever came its way.

Again, hissing evilly through the water came its sibilant whisper: "*Hra . . . le . . . ka . . . na.*"

Everything that sank into the Deep eventually came down to it, where it lay in the very sewer of the world. Whole fleets of wooden ships—rotten, scarcely recognizable—lay crumbling in its coils. Their treasures spilled across the floor of the ocean in dully glittering dunes that the tentacles writhed over and swept into ever new shapes. And ships of iron, too, old steamers and ocean liners. I watched a tentacle clutch and lift a warship with a dark hole in its belly and shake it like a rattle, its heavy insides thudding, *Boom Boom Boom*.

Under the monster's evershifting tentacles, I saw fragments of human dwellings stretching for leagues—walls with images formed of colored stones, and broken columns crusted over with shellfish. These were the ruins of a vast city, with buildings once fathoms high that had collapsed under the Kraken's weight or in some primeval catastrophe. I wondered if this whole pit had once been part of a land that sank toward the center of the earth.

Between these ruins I saw white reefs in fantastic shapes. I wondered how coral could live at this depth, till I realized that the skulls and bones of humans made up these gruesome compositions. The bones of those lost with the ships settled down here and were swept into piles by the always restless tentacles, where they calcified like the tiny shells of coral animals in the lagoons. I wondered, with a shudder, what had stripped the flesh from them. Here and there among them lay the skeleton of a walrus, whale, or other sea creature.

Such was the lair of the Kraken, and again its whisper moved over me like a stream of putrid water:

"*Hra . . . le . . . ka . . . na.*"

Under the restless tentacles clouds of murk and sand stirred and settled, and dark debris rose from the floor and traveled in foul currents before settling again. I heard the loud rush of water passing through the creature's gills and recognized the source of the sound I had heard in the tunnel. I felt the current push against me and then pull me toward the abominable inhaler of these waters. Occasionally a smell unutterably foul—the essence of all dead things—assaulted me as the current pulled with peculiar force. In addition to the whisper of its breathing, I now and again heard a horrible grinding and gnashing as the gigantic beak, somewhere among its curling legs, closed, *DOOM DOOM*, on an object and ground it to pieces.

For this was, after all, the Kraken, the immense sea monster prophesied from the first to rise at the last day in its death agony to wreak destruction on the ocean and the land. As one of our ancient prophets sang,

> *Below the thunder of the upper deep,*
> *Far, far beneath in the abysmal sea,*
> *His ancient, dreamless, uninvaded sleep*
> *The Kraken sleeps . . .*
>
> *There has he lain for ages, and will lie*
> *Battening upon huge sea worms in his sleep,*
> *Until the latter fire shall heat the deep;*
> *Then once by man and whales to be seen,*
> *In roaring he shall rise and on the surface die.*

I remembered in the vision of the beginning of things how the dark star had cast a shadow into the Deep. Whether the Kraken was that shadow or one of his perverse offspring made little difference to me now: for the dread of him was upon me.

I cried out—to the Whale of Light—for my flesh quaked with fear and revulsion. I cried out to the presence that brought me down the tunnel.

But there was no answer.

Now, between the closings of that horrible beak, I heard the whisper again, the mumbled words and singsong, and my heart recoiled as they came clear:

> *Come closer, come closer, I know you're here.*
> *I've waited for you for many a year.*
> *On your sweet bones I'll grind my beak—*
> *Just one swift bite will end your fear.*

Without a pause he began again,

> *Come closer, come closer, I know you're here.*
> *I've waited for you for many a year . . .*

repeating the singsong over and over until my head pounded with it.

There was no other answer to my cry. Only silence, followed by the slow, idiotic whisper.

Drained of strength, I didn't flee back up the tunnel. Though abandoned and sick at heart, I knew I must go out and meet the monster. For this purpose I had come.

Chapter Three

As if I didn't have trouble enough, my wound started throbbing again. The blood had flowed ever more freely as I came down the tunnel, but I'd ignored it. Now the pain returned as I felt the jagged piece of metal in it move.

But I had to ignore the pain and move out from the cover of the tunnel under the baleful eye of the Kraken. I felt utterly alone. Gone was the presence that had given me confidence as I traveled down the tunnel. I clung to the few words I had been told: that I must go forward boldly to meet what lay at the bottom; that its worst enemy was any deed selflessly done; and, most mysterious of all, that my wound would be my weapon.

But it was hard to hold on to these words in the presence of the Kraken. They seemed empty and foolhardy. Here was no foe I could do battle with in any way I knew, no squid such as Hrūna struggled with, flipper to tentacle, and triumphed over. I was smaller than any one of the Kraken's tentacles. Attacking the monster would be like attacking a continent.

Feeling small and exposed, I moved out toward the cold, searching light of the Kraken's eyes. As I did, the pain increased. I had no heart left and did not sing my battle song, for to do so seemed utter folly. But under my breath I repeated to myself, "Courage shall the keener be as my might dwindles," though the words sounded hollow and weak.

I caught the flickering light of the Kraken's gaze. Its eyes swelled blindingly as they focused on me. A lurid laugh underlay its idiotic rhyme, which it repeated as if trying to hypnotize me. To resist the rhyme, I sang to myself.

And then, all at once, it didn't matter what happened to me. I felt a strange freedom and lightness of heart. I almost laughed. Whatever grip I could get on one of those tentacles, I would do my utmost, using fluke and flipper to strike and baleen to bite until the end.

To my surprise, the Kraken did not send its tentacles rushing toward me. Rather it pulled them back under itself. For a foolish moment I thought it might be retreating from me, and I swam boldly toward it—over the heaps of treasure, broken ships, and reefs of bone.

For a moment the Kraken was silent. With no idea what I would do next, I rushed at it. A second later, I stopped. Echoing from a thousand cliffs came the hideous roar of the monster, like a hundred volcanoes erupting at once, like the Ice at the End of the World splitting in half. The cliffs re-echoed with its cry, and the water vibrated and shook until I could not move.

I saw the Kraken gather its legs under itself and spring like a white and evil dawn into the blackness above, covering half the pit, its legs swirling and writhing around its immense perimeter like waterspouts in a typhoon.

Even if I tried to return to the tunnel, I would never make it. I knew my duty was to await the attack, and I stayed steady near the floor of that vast pit.

The Kraken covered me like an evil sky—a sickly gray cloud stretching from cliff to cliff, its tentacles writhing around me. I saw right above me, in the center of its legs, the enormous black beak opening and closing, *Doom Doom,* revealing a ghastly white mouth and stomach behind the choppers. Slowly, leisurely, it descended on me.

26

I saw its outsized advantage, its huge bullying bulk, and that made me angry. I put all I had into a roar that near the surface would have resounded for miles, but here sounded puny, muted by the acres of flesh above me. I shot straight up toward the writhing beak.

It opened wide to receive me.

At the last instant, I swerved to the left and rammed with all my force the soft underbelly of the Kraken. The blow knocked me dizzy and I saw spots. The Kraken was caught by surprise, for it recoiled a few yards and hesitated a moment while I regained my wits. Then it opened its beak again and moved down on me.

Doom Doom, the beak gnashed, opening fathoms wide, each half like a black granite slab. Even more terrifying was what shone through these deadly gates. In its maw, phosphorescent with decay, lay the remains of its victims and the carrion it sucked from the bottom of the sea. A putrid odor assaulted me, of dead flesh, burned oil, and other poisons. I felt, too, the Invisible Burning, as if all things decaying and destructive were filtered from the water by this bloated bottomfeeder.

I saw the empty eyesockets of those it had taken from the ships that lay crushed on the heap beneath it. I knew now that the glowing putrescence was the source of the Kraken's light, that it irradiated every limb of the squid and gave it its deathly illumination.

I was afraid, but shook the fear from me, for the Whale of Light had told me the Kraken could devour nothing that was good—nothing *living* and good.

I backed up, once again, to charge the soft underbelly, when I felt something slimy wrap around me and the sting of giant suction disks fastening themselves to my skin.

My flippers pinned to my sides, I couldn't move. I thrashed with my flukes and made some headway, but the tentacle squeezed tighter. A hideous laugh filled the water all about me. While the tentacle squeezed, my wound throbbed with a sickening pain.

"So," the Kraken breathed, and I couldn't tell where its voice, hollow and ghostly, came from. "*You have come to me at last! I waited long, but never thought you would come so willingly and try to throw yourself into my mouth. You've made it almost too easy,*" it hissed. "*But first, I must see you clearly.*"

At those words, the long tentacle swung out from under the Kraken and lifted me up before its eyes, which were empty but lit with a baleful light.

Then the laugh erupted—a nasty, echoing laugh, hoarse and wretched, ending in an insane snigger. The white spotted miles of flesh shook, puckered, and writhed in unholy glee.

"*To think,*" the voice continued, "*that the ancient verse says this is what I am to fear!*" And it thundered and quaked with laughter again.

"*What can you say for yourself, you. . . you white sardine?*" the Kraken breathed, oozing contempt. But I had resolved to say nothing and I clenched my jaws to prevent a word from escaping.

The Kraken shook me and grew angry. "*Speak!*" it screamed. "*Or I shall squeeze you to jelly.*" The coil tightened, but I remained silent.

The coil constricted again and I resisted with all my strength. I stared fixedly into those pale eyes while light and shadow passed over them like storms over a turbulent sea. While I stared, the Kraken drew back slightly, and its grip loosened a little.

All at once I was struck by an overwhelming sense of loneliness in an ocean of darkness, as if I'd entered into the Kraken's thoughts. I felt a strange sympathy for this monstrosity, alone here at the bottom of the sea. The feeling flooded me like a tidal wave: an immense self-pity. *Alone, alone,* it seemed to echo, *and all are against me.* The whole universe appeared indifferent, inexpressibly weary and ugly. The very light pressed down on me like a weight.

I wondered why I had bothered to struggle with this great Wretchedness before me. What harm had it done me, after all? It had been treated unfairly. I felt irritated that I had been sent down here to disturb it, and the weariness of the effort overwhelmed me. All my muscles went slack.

At that instant I felt the coil constrict to squeeze the breath out of me, and I realized it was a trick: The Kraken had attacked my mind with its own miasmal mood, and I'd almost given up. Alarmed and angry, I stretched every sinew, trying to wriggle from the serpentine grasp. Wrath flared in the pale eyes before me.

"So be it," the Kraken roared. *"Then I shall finish you off right away. I am hungry."*

The tentacle swung me down under toward the huge beak, which clacked open and shut in anticipation, *Doom, Doom.* Larger and larger it loomed, the water from it fetid.

"So this is it," I thought, but strained every muscle to escape. Expanding my chest as much as possible, I threw my flukes to the left and pushed with my flippers just as the tentacle loosened its grip to toss me into the giant mouth. In one swift twist I broke free and darted aside. The tentacles writhed about me, tangling with each other, and I felt a powerful current. The Kraken was sucking water into its mouth in an effort to pull me in. I swam with all my might against the current, thrashing aside the confusion of tentacles. But it was too strong for me, and inch by inch, tail first, I was sucked toward the gaping beak.

I glanced back. The blood was streaming from my wound into its maw. The suction was too great; I could not hold out much longer. I thought of Aleea waiting above, and Lewtë and Hrūna, and tried to picture the smile of the Whale of Light, when I felt a wrenching and tearing in my side.

Glancing back, I saw a piece of metal slip from my wound, jagged and sharp, and turn end over end as it was sucked back into the writhing mouth. It appeared to glow, whether from the dismal light of the Kraken or not, I cannot say. The gleaming fragment passed between the halves of the cruel beak, which snapped shut with a loud *Doom*.

In the brief cessation of current, I slipped between two tentacles groping for me. I was nearly out from under the monster when I heard a loud rumble and the whole sky of flesh above me began to quake. A head-splitting shriek pierced the water and an inky black cloud descended, putrid and impenetrable, blinding me. Tentacles thrashed, groping about in the murk. I dove to the bottom and, hugging it, wove among the ruins and bones, finding my way by echo toward the tunnel, expecting any instant a tentacle to grab me from behind.

I heard the Kraken screaming with pain and anger and a growing thunder as its tentacles thrashed, tearing up rocks and wrecks looking for me, pulling at the cliffs around the pit, setting off avalanches in its wrath, and beating against the bottom, trying to smash me. Fortunately, its own ink, released to confuse me when it tasted the metal, provided cover for my way back to the cliff.

At last I reached the tunnel, while the Kraken's cries grew ever more angry and shrill. I swam up it a short distance before looking back. There in its nest, writhing, its eyes flashing every which way with a malignant brilliance, I saw the earthshaker move. It screamed with rage and thrashed everywhere, seeking the one who had brought it pain, the metal cutting at its vitals. It writhed and convulsed, trying to regurgitate the fragment, while it rotated in a frenzy, tearing at itself and at the cliffs, bringing down stone in avalanches that shook the foundations of the Deep.

That was the last I saw of it, for guessing I was in the tunnel, the Kraken thrust one tentacle up into it. I turned and fled, hearing behind me a cry of rage and despair, a wail of such hopelessness as I wished never to hear again. The fat tentacle squeezed in a short way, then withdrew and beat against the cliff face. With a loud crack, the cliff collapsed, blocking that end of the tunnel forever. Afraid the rest would collapse, I fled up into the darkness, feeling the water grow cool again.

I kept on, though my wound throbbed and my ribs ached from the crush of the huge tentacle, and my skin burned, rubbed raw by the suction cups. I knew I was losing blood fast, but somehow I didn't care, for the piece of metal was gone from my wound forever, swallowed by the Kraken.

Then the thought struck me, and I stopped cold, as the meaning of the Whale of Light's words came over me: *The Kraken can devour nothing good*, and *Your wound shall be your weapon*.

It was wonderfully silent around me, but far below, from the earth's center, came the rumble of earthquake and ruin.

As I swam up into the cold water, the noises behind me faded. Best of all, I no longer heard the Kraken's whisper, with its idiotic rhyme, nor felt the water move with the monster's breathing. The waters were still and sweet, and I swam up into the silence.

No longer did I feel alone. There was a presence all about me, and it was as if the waters rang with some unheard music, a chorus beyond the farthest reach of hearing.

I was content to move up into the stillness, free of fear, anxiety, and even expectation. There in the darkness I had a vision. I noticed the water grow lighter and, glancing to each side, I saw two brilliant creatures, all of light, escorting me. They glided effortlessly alongside me, their gaze fixed on something I could not see. They sang and, as they sang, I felt a tingling warmth. The pain from my wounds was disappearing. That from my bruised ribs vanished first, and then the abrasions from the Kraken's suckers. The blood from my side slowed, and the pain from the metal shard lessened. How long they swam beside me, I do not know, but suddenly I was rising in the dark again, except for a faint glow in the water immediately surrounding me.

At long last I emerged from the upper end of the tunnel into a Deep that was only a shade lighter. Feeling renewed from head to tail, I climbed slowly up the abyss until I saw the dim entrance to Hralekana's cavern.

I entered it, turning around as before to face the opening. There I rested, repeating the word to myself. Over and over I silently invoked it until I felt so much at peace my recent adventure seemed almost a dream.

I do not know how long I stayed there, for I may have slept. But a moment came when I was rested and in possession of my full strength. I knew it was time to return to those on the surface.

When I rose above the waves, it was early dawn and I breathed out, my spout making a gold spray in the mist. No one was about. I had the sea to myself, and the air was fresh and sweet. I rolled over in it and drank in the cries of curlews and the smells of early morning.

I spyhopped, scanning the horizon, and glimpsed the telltale spouts of Aleea and Lewtë, who were foraging for food. Hrūna was nowhere to be seen. I was glad to have caught them off guard.

Diving, I swam in a wide circle around Aleea and Lewtë, approaching them from the east. I came up behind them, where they were feeding on the surface. The rising sun was directly behind me.

"Be well!" I hailed them as any friendly passing whale might, altering my voice. "Why are the two of you alone in these waters?"

Aleea squinted into the sun, trying to see me. She choked and her eyes shone with tears.

"Stranger, has no one told you what has happened in these waters? How two days ago we carried here the best of all whales, with a mortal wound in his side, and watched as he sank far below to the cave of Hralekana?"

"Oh—" my mother Lewtë joined her, the oil of tears in her eyes, "how we still hoped he would revive, for from that cave we heard his voice rising. That indeed was the cruelest of hopes, because it came to mock our grief. Those whose hearts had been pierced by his approaching death experienced a false dawn. For after a while his voice faded, then ceased altogether. . . . We fear the worst."

"Now we wait," Aleea said, trembling with grief. "And we do not know what we wait for. For by his last words he forbade us to descend to the cave to be with him, even in his death. And this last is the hardest of all to bear."

At that, I thought I saw a puzzled look cross Lewtë's face, but Aleea was blinded by tears.

Unable to bear it any longer, I swam up to Aleea and said in my own voice, "Aleea, don't you know who it is that speaks?"

She looked at me a long second through her tears and let out a cry like a mortal wound of gladness. It shook me to the depths and was instantly joined by another from Lewtë.

"Hralekana?" Aleea asked in disbelief, moving closer. She stared for a moment, paralyzed, then seized me between her flippers, as did Lewtë from behind, and we rolled, the three of us, churning the surface.

Suddenly they drew back, and Aleea said in a small voice, "At first I thought it was the sunlight on you, but there is light coming from you."

"Have no fear," I said. "It is still I, your old playfellow." Then the three of us rolled like herring in a bubble net and thrashed the water to foam, sending spout after spout sparkling in the rising sun.

Our cries alerted Hrūna, miles away in pursuit of a pod of sharks that had circled the three. Approaching, he heard Aleea and Lewtë singing, for they could not contain themselves.

"Hralekana!" Hrūna's loud voice interrupted them, shaking through the water as he sped toward us. He paused several lengths away and exclaimed, "I can't believe my eyes. Is it really you?" While we embraced, he touched me all over to make sure I was really there and in one piece. He discovered the wound, which was still bleeding slightly, and swam down to look at it. The other two joined him. Their faces fell.

"Don't be alarmed," I said. "It no longer pains me nor causes any weakness. I feel better now than ever in my life."

"I can see that, my son," Hrūna said softly, "but where did these marks come from?" With his flipper he traced three enormous circular scars on my back and sides. "Except for these marks and the wound, your skin is as clean as a newborn calf's. There's not a barnacle on you anywhere."

The three looked at me with a mixture of awe and curiosity.

"We have much to talk about," I said, "which we will do shortly. But first, where are the herring? I'm famished."

Chapter Four

The sun's golden head was well above the horizon when we four turned into its flashing track, heading east to meet the pod on their way south. We guessed how far along they'd be on the annual journey, slowed down as they were by the new calves. It was a fresh spring morning on those open seas, with a stiff gale blowing spindrift off the whitecaps. The troughs between the waves shone lustrous green, the sky, blue. The whole world was made new. Yet something about our course bothered me.

"Can the pod have come this far south?" I asked Hrūna.

"Yes, my son. You forget that a second dawn passed while you were under the waves. This is the third day since you sank into the Deep."

I said nothing for a long while.

As we swam east, the sun climbed overhead and finally dropped behind us, sinking into a bank of clouds streaked red. We heard the pod long before we saw them. At last, spouts appeared on the horizon, glowing pink in the light from the west. So did their high splashes as they leaped in the traditional greeting.

The three swam on ahead while I hung back. When they'd nearly reached the others, I dove into the Black Deep before angling up toward the pod. From far below I saw them clustered, black and tiny, against the silver sky, while they questioned Aleea, Hrūna, and Lewtë. From the Deep they looked small and unprotected, like a school of minnows, and I felt a rush of love for them.

I aimed right for the middle of the pod, taking on speed as I rose. Eagerly listening to Aleea and Hrūna, none saw me rise. The sky, wrinkling and shaking through the water, rushed closer. Suddenly I was above it in the longest, smoothest leap I'd ever made. Higher and higher I climbed into a light blue sky covered with salmon-tinted clouds. I reached out with my flippers and saw drops flash from their edges as I rose into the sun. For a moment, I wondered if, like the whale who loved a star, I would head up through the clouds into the starlit vastness of space. But I curved over onto my back, and glancing down, saw the others looking up in shock.

I hung there a moment, arched over on my back, then dropped down smoothly onto water reflecting the salmon clouds. A wall of white water erupted on all sides as I sank and rolled over, righting myself in the foam. While the waves settled, the pod rocked and flailed, rushing in to greet me: Grandfather Hrunta, Grandmother Hreelëa, my friend Hrekka, and even old Hrobo the Singer—so gray and mottled with barnacles he was almost white—crowded in to press flipper, fluke, and side against me.

I rolled, and they rolled. We made a noisy melee of grunts, clicks, whistles, and spoutings, and the new calves squealed and leaped over my back, splashing all and sundry.

Then everyone drew back in a large circle, staring. It was old Hrobo who spoke first: "Welcome home, Hralekana-kolua, whom we never thought to see again." And then, with a low hum moving in from the outer fringes of the pod, they began to sing:

> *Wide is the ocean, and far is the wandering*
> *That takes one from us, side from warm side.*

Great is the gulf that brings on the darkness
And cold the night harpooned by the stars.

Long are the tears and echoless the crying
When love lies waiting for love returning.
But fresh in the morning beyond all dreaming
From the Deep he rises, warm side to warm side.

That night in the thin light of a crescent moon we lay, softly bumping against each other in sleep. Now and then I woke to feel the reassuring warmth of Aleea and hear the little waves lapping against the dark, gleaming sides circled about the sleeping calves, or hear the stertorous clicking and wheezing of old Hrobo, snoring to the sea rhythms of his songs.

During one of these times Aleea woke too, and we swam out under the dim moon, alone. The sea was still, and a few stars glittered on the surface.

"I thought I had lost you for good," Aleea said, her voice wavering. I couldn't say anything for a while. The white star on her forehead glimmered in the moon. I recalled the first time I saw it, as a calf, and nudged it, gently stroking the white stripe down her side.

"In the hours after the wound," I said, "while you and Hrūna were carrying me along, I somehow knew I must go to Hralekana's cavern. I didn't know why." A breeze passed over us and rocked the reflected stars.

Aleea pressed closer: "When you sank there, I wanted to sink with you. When your voice stopped, I felt the life drain from me. Afterward I was numb. And then this morning . . ." She pushed her head under my flipper and tears came.

I told her how I had come to in the cave and been led down the dark tunnel. I told her of some of my Seeings and that I had been healed in that darkness, though I did not understand how. I said nothing about the Kraken, however.

The moon came out from behind a cloud and cast a jagged track across the waters. I pressed against Aleea. She laughed and rolled, flashing toward the moon. I chased after her, and we played, looping and breaching in those moon-tickled seas until the dawn blushed in the east.

The next day was given over to games and celebration, which allowed the mothers and calves to rest and gather fresh strength for the journey. The games, songs, and acrobatics went on in friendly and hilarious rivalry as we chased the Red Bull of the Sun and later the White Cow of the Moon across the sky.

Together Hrūna and I invented a new game for the calves, launching them into the air with our flukes and catching them. Dizzy with flying, they returned again and again, shrieking like sea gulls for more. That second night we slept soundly, tired from the games and ready to journey again toward the Ice at the End of the World. I woke once, troubled by a dream in which I saw the starving whale of my vision. The thin whale was trying to breach but could barely lift his face above the water. His skull showed through the skin. I woke and was comforted by the soft breathing of Aleea at my side and the rumble of Hrobo's snore. Nevertheless, I knew we must not delay any longer our search for krill.

The remaining days passed swiftly as we neared the Pole. Once again we passed close to Hralekana's cavern. As the waters grew colder, everyone swam with new vigor.

It wasn't long before the first ice floe floated by and then, surrounded by mist, a tall iceberg. The new calves stared at it wide-eyed. I circled it with them and the larger ones dove with me to watch its huge underwater shape turn through the sea.

While we watched it, I told them the story of the iron monster that challenged an ice mountain on the far side of the world and how the monster sank into the Deep. I told them of that other iron monster filled with black oil that had struck the ice wall last year and how the serpent of oil crawled forth and poisoned our food. I also told them of the iron monsters with red and green eyes that hunted us and for which we must keep watch in these waters. At this, many of them grew too quiet, so I told them the tale of the whale who loved a star and had them all practice breaching—to see, I said, if any could leap as high as the top of the ice mountain.

That afternoon the white edge of the Ice at the End of the World rose over the horizon. Even I felt the calves' excitement as the harsh and wild music of the ice grew loud where the icebergs broke loose and jostled toward the open sea. Soon, we passed by the islands of the birds, now strangely silent. There were no bird nests, where last year there had been hundreds. And no birds. The beaches were black with tar from the oil spilled the year before.

But the biggest surprise of the journey lay ahead. When we came to the place where the krill beds normally stretched for miles, turning the waters pinkish orange, we found nothing. Nothing but empty water as far as the eye could see. A cry went up from the hungry mothers, followed by shrill wailing from the young and groans and clickings from the fathers. My dream had been a warning that the krill was gone.

While we stared at the empty water, three dark spots rose over the ice, heading toward us.

A squawk of delight rang out. I recognized Ross's voice as his whitened and restored wings beat madly and he landed on my nose with a thump, nearly losing his balance and tumbling off into the sea. Moments later his parents, Ala and Ali, circled over Hrūna and Lewtë and alighted gracefully on their backs.

"Glad!" Ross burst out, breathless. "Glad . . . you're . . . here." He stopped, beak open, his breast feathers puffing up and down like foam in a wild surf. The pod laughed.

Ross was the albatross friend I'd grown up with during summers at the Pole, a big clumsy fellow with a wingspread as long as my flipper. For years we'd hunted and played together. Ala, Ali, and Ross served as the eyes of the pod, helping us feed safely while they watched for whalers and Killer whales. Last year Ross had fallen into the oil and nearly suffocated.

He walked around my blowhole three times, stretching his wings and folding them till he caught his breath. I remembered his feeble scrabblings and twitchings after he nearly drowned in the oil and was glad for his solid step and the way his toes dug into my hide.

Finally he said, "All of the krill are not gone. An hour's swim from here is what remains of the bed—not very much, but fresh and clean of all trace of oil." He pecked my blowhole affectionately and I blasted him with my hot breath, knocking him off balance. Ala and Ali confirmed the news, and the Council quickly decided to inspect what was left.

The next morning the pod swam silently to the west, the three albatrosses leading us. Ross perched by my blowhole and told us about the lean winter at the Pole, how the ships had left before the oil broke up on shore, coating much of the ice and clinging in tarry dregs to the rocks. Although the humans in the small yellow ship and others had worked for weeks rescuing gulls, terns, shearwaters, penguins, and otters, many more animals had died in the sludge. Their silent bodies floated for weeks afterward covered with tar, bumping in mute protest against oil-covered rocks or lying along the beach in the shapes of their last agony.

The fish, finding their food destroyed, had moved away from shore, and it had been a lean winter for the birds that remained, including the albatrosses. Most of the krill were caught in the serpentine oil and, smothered, sank to the bottom.

Before Ross finished his account, I saw a slight riffle on the surface a mile away. "Krill!" someone called out, and we sped to where the water shone the familiar orange of millions of tiny shrimp swimming together in a mass. Several of the mothers plunged into the bed before Hrūna cried, "Stop!" Embarrassed, they backed out.

The rest of us lay there stunned. Rather than stretching beyond sight as in the old days, the krill bed was entirely visible from where we lay. It reached barely a quarter of a mile in any direction, and the krill extended to only a few feet below the surface.

Everyone was quiet for a long time. At last Hrūna spoke: "What we see is only a remnant of the old krill bed. It amounts to no more than what the pod can swallow in one day. Though we feel now the hunger from a whole year without krill, we must not consume these few that are left."

A faint wail rose from the mothers of the new calves.

"We must not, and yet there are those among us who will soon starve without such food. So this is what I propose to the Council: Each new mother and her calf may feed for one day. The yearlings, too. The rest of us must wait for them at a distance, lest the frenzy of feeding overwhelm us."

A great hollow space in me made itself known. To smell the fresh shrimp in the water and not be able to eat it made me feel like one huge hunger inside. That lush salad in which I had lost myself each summer of my life, feeding for days without care, tunneling through the shrimp, was now to be backed off from! I saw the same feeling in the others' faces. There was another look, too, a look of fear that if we didn't find another krill bed soon, some would starve before the season was over.

At a signal, the six new mothers and their calves plunged into the krill, joined by the yearlings, more ravenous than any. We watched their flukes vanish into the delicious orange mass. At a whistle from Hrūna, the rest of us turned and, without glancing back, swam a mile to the ice.

I saw a hollow look in Aleea's eye, and as we swam away, her eyes misted over.

"What is wrong?" I asked, alarmed.

"Nothing—" she said, "except . . . that I wanted to tell you at a happier time."

"Tell me what?"

She looked at me and smiled shyly through her tears, and all at once I knew. "A calf?" I cried, scarcely able to believe it. "A calf!" And then I hugged her and rolled until we raised a cyclone of waves.

"It *is* a happy time!" I exclaimed when we stopped, and I gave out a triumphant bellow that echoed from the ice a dozen times. Others swam up to hear the news. Ala, Ali, and Ross flapped and shrieked, flying in a wild circle above us.

At this glad news the pod forgot their hunger, and we played and sported as if we were back in tropical seas. Hrekka, Hrūna, and I breached three times together and lobtailed until the sounds echoed like thunder from the ice wall, shaking loose an ice slide or two.

But amid the excitement, another thought struck me—Aleea needed food for two now. I pushed her toward the krill, though she needed little pushing. As she entered the shrinking krill bed, I thought how we needed to find more krill or else Aleea and our unborn calf might starve. I swam slowly back to the pod, trying to shut that thought from my mind. For the remainder of that afternoon the pod rested, waiting for the mothers and calves to finish feeding.

When she was done, Aleea and I went off alone, almost too happy to speak.

Finally I said, "I wish Mark were here to tell."

Aleea smiled. "He'd be spinning in the water, knowing his saving you from the sea pond had led to this."

I thought of our kindly human friend—thin, all flippers and no fat, with his bony, divided flukes and his blue removable skin. Picturing him aboard the yellow *Rainbow Whale*, perhaps even now sailing between the dangerous warships, I felt a rush of affection for him. I hoped that somehow he could feel it over the bend of the earth's waters.

That night the Council met to determine what the pod should do. The next morning, with the albatrosses flying ahead as our eyes, we swam west, circling toward the far side of the Pole where we knew more krill lay. It would be a journey of many days, but we had no choice.

On the afternoon of the second day we heard strange noises in the distance. First came the high-pitched whistles of a school of tuna, punctuated by the cries of dolphins in distress. These were joined by a variety of cries, including those of a seal, a Minke whale, and a Fin whale.

The three albatrosses flew back to us at great speed, low over the water.

"Ships!" Ala announced, "Whalers, small ships. They have nets out many miles long and are taking everything—fish, dolphins, small whales and large—that becomes trapped in them, even terns and gulls."

A slow chill moved through us as we heard this. In the past, the whalers had used only harpoons. Now they were using nets for whales like those of the fishers I saw the year before.

While the pod waited, five of us from the Council swam ahead to investigate. If this was a large fleet of whalers, with echo finders, we would not be able to pass that way.

The cries grew louder and more numerous as black bumps on the horizon took the shape of iron monsters. We tasted fear in the water. We counted seven of the monsters of various shapes and sizes, but we saw no large mother ship. This was not the whaling fleet we knew from the past.

"Pirate whalers," I said, and Hrūna grunted agreement. None had seen so many in one place before. Usually each hunted alone. From where we watched, we saw the pirate whalers doing a number of strange things. Two of them were drawing in nets, winding them around big iron logs on their tails. Men were removing fish and birds caught in the nets and throwing them into the water, where many floated, stunned.

Soon we saw what they were after. We heard a wild bark as they drew up a black, shiny shape. It was a seal. The seal wriggled out of the net onto the deck. The men made a pass at him with a noose and missed. Two lunged for him, but he shook them off, nipping one on the arm. The man cried out and leaped back. With a defiant bark the seal flopped over the stern of the ship and swam away.

Meanwhile, behind the second ship with a net the water was churning. There, wrapped twice around by the net, was a large Fin whale thrashing and trying to escape. Men in small boats put out from the ship, carrying what looked like thundersticks and harpoons. While we watched, the Fin surged with a loud cry of anger and broke the net, swimming away with it trailing after him. The five of us sang out in triumph.

Still, alarmed by what we'd seen, we turned back. The albatrosses wheeled above us and the sun clouded over as we swam, considering our situation. Suddenly Ross cried out. One of the boats had started toward us; its sharp bow cut wings on the water. We heard the *ping* of its echo finder. Without a word, we dove to the bottom and spread out, away from the pod and toward the ice.

Later we gathered at the edge of the ice shelf. We couldn't see or hear the ship; the albatrosses said it had turned back once its *ping* lost touch with us. We dared not try to pass by these murderous pirates with their echo finders and small, fast ships. They'd stop at nothing to get at us, setting traps with their long nets in which we would drown as they dragged us in. Not even a calf was safe from them. Yet the other way around the Pole, to the east, was longer. Already hungry, the pod could starve before we finished that journey.

Nevertheless, by the time we reached the others, we'd decided to go east. We had no other choice.

Chapter Five

With anxious faces the pod received news of the pirate whalers. Some had already gathered much from the baleful sounds that traveled through the water. We told what we had seen, stressing the danger of the nets. But everyone was delighted at the story of the seal's escape.

Faces grew grim when Hrūna told of the Council's decision to go east. The mothers and young calves were hungry again, despite yesterday's krill. But after murmuring and grumbling, the pod swung about and headed back the way we'd come.

The next day we paused again at the shrunken remnant of krill so that mothers and calves—and those cows with calf—might feed one last time. The rest of us were allowed a few mouthfuls. On the following day we left our familiar feeding ground and the bare islands and steered east into a bank of fog. We moved by echo, following the ice shelf, on the alert for iron monsters. The albatrosses flew invisibly above the fog, which they reported covered ice and sea. We cried back and forth to each other.

In the afternoon the sun shone weakly through a break in the fog. In these new waters the ice shelf was mountainous and huge. The fog swirled and parted, revealing an icy cliff shining with a dismal sheen, and closed again. Three shadows crossed the white disk of the sun and flew down to rest. There were no more breaks in sight.

That night we slept close to the ice, members of the Council taking turns keeping watch. The fog was so thick that nothing in the water or above it was visible. Fog dripped from the points of ice thrusting out over our heads. In the middle of the night I woke to hear the groans and roaring thunder of the ice making mournful music as it slid into the sea. The fog had partially lifted and a wan half-moon shone over the ice above us, shrouding it in eerie light. Several huge bergs broke off at a distance and the ice wall above us quivered in sympathy, making a ringing sound.

I woke the others, and we moved out toward the open sea. Just in time, too. A cracking sound, many times louder than a harpoon going off, split the bay, and we watched the ice wall behind us dissolve in an avalanche, collapsing into the sea in sparkling pieces while a plume of mist rose to the moon.

Three dark shapes flapped shrieking down through the plume to see if we were all right. All three albatrosses had been sleeping on the top of the cliff when their perch suddenly gave way under them.

Too excited to go back to sleep, we swam through the night, lit fitfully by the moon overhead. The ice continued its strange symphony of moans, cracks, and howls as the great bergs jostled and turned away from the frozen land of their birth.

The dawn came, faintly pink, and though the fog was gone, the clouds soon closed over us without a break. Traveling along that icy coast made us nervous, partly because of the unusual silence. There were very few birds—an occasional gull or plover was all. Nor had we seen any seals, walruses, or other animals in this direction. The reason wasn't far to seek. On some of the ice and rocky islands lay telltale marks of last year's oil. We hadn't known that the spill was so wide, that the winds had pushed it so far east.

The pod's pace had slowed and some of the younger calves were giving out, having to be carried by the adults. The mothers were visibly thinner, unable to replenish their milk. Nevertheless, we made headway without incident over the next few days.

One morning I saw a silver cloud flash through the sea far to port. Herring—the first we'd seen in these waters. I lunged to the left, the rest of the pod after me. As the school of herring wove and shimmered near the surface, Aleea and I dove under it and released a ring of bubbles, driving the fish together. We drew the bubble net tight until the mothers and calves arrived. They filled themselves with the delicacy before the others joined in the feast.

There were glad cries from the young, who had not fed since the krill. They leaped and splashed on the surface.

"Look at them leap!" Aleea said, having finished feeding. She nuzzled me. "It's as if I can already feel the calf inside me leaping too." I pressed against her, and we rolled slowly over, resting under a sky blue for that one afternoon.

A few days later, the sky white above us, we saw Ala hurrying from the east. Ross was napping on my back. At his father's cry, he snapped awake and leaped into the air to meet him. Ala didn't pause but flew straight to Hrūna's back.

The pod gathered around as he caught his breath. He looked at us gravely and said, "The whaling fleet is just over the horizon. I've never seen it so large, more than twice ten iron monsters. There are different colors waving from their tails. I think different pods of humans are on board."

"Can we swim between them and the ice?" Hrūna asked, his voice anxious.

Ala lifted a black foot and put it down, staring at it. "I'm afraid the ships are waiting in a line from right next to the ice far into the ocean. To go around them, you'd have to swim miles out to sea, far from the protection of the ice."

As before, the Council swam ahead to look over the fleet. An hour's swimming brought us in view of the largest whaling fleet we'd ever seen. I counted over a dozen iron monsters with harpoons on their noses and two of the white mother monsters with jaws that swallowed a whale whole. These factory ships loomed large, with many eyes on their tops and sides, ghastly in the light of an overcast sky. None of the catchers was chasing anything. They lay in a long line, stretching out into the ocean as far as the eye could see. Each circled slowly in place as if waiting for something.

Now and then we heard the distant *pings* of an echo finder. While the ships circled, their tails flapped with various colors. This giant whaling fleet looked as if it was made up of several smaller fleets that often hunted in these waters.

We saw no signs of the nets used by the pirate whalers to the west. Yet the fleet's lying in a long line was strange and blocked our journey east. We heard the churn and grinding of metal inside the ships and the slow *thrug thrug* of the giant screws that pushed them through the water. The red and green eyes on either side and the many white eyes along their tops appeared to search the sea for us. Louder came the faint *pings* from their listening ears.

Without a word we turned and dove, taking a roundabout way back to the pod in case any catcher followed us.

"The way east is blocked," Hrūna told the pod, a look of great worry in his eyes. A low wail went up, a keening as if someone had died. Hrūna paused until it faded away.

"Will we have to go west again?" one of the calves asked, his voice thin and choked.

"No," Hrūna said, "we cannot go back that way, for the pirate whalers block it."

"Then let us go back to the remainder of the krill," said one of the cows, her voice a hoarse whisper.

"They would last us only three days," Hrūna said, no emotion showing in his voice. "Then we would have nothing and be no better off."

"But a little is better than nothing," my friend Hrekka said.

"There is another way." Hrūna said, glancing at him sharply. "A dangerous way, but it is our only choice."

I knew what he referred to, for he and I had already discussed it.

The others pressed closer.

Hrūna cleared his throat. "You all know how in the past we have fled under the ice when danger threatened and found safety in open lagoons among the great ice mountains. The distances to them were short, and even the calves could hold their breath long enough.

"Behind the icebergs there is the ice shelf, which we've always ventured under more carefully, for the open water there is limited to small air holes kept open by the seals. Many a whale, losing his way and missing the air holes or finding them frozen over, has drowned under the ice shelf."

Here he paused, while mothers looked anxiously at calves and we all shivered, recalling stories we'd heard.

"Unfortunately, our only chance to pass the whalers is to travel under the ice shelf, for it extends out from land all the way to the other side of the Pole. Here and there the icebergs cluster against it and offer less dangerous shelter, but there are immense stretches where only the ice shelf can cover us.

"We will need to swim under the ice from air hole to air hole. Now and then, perhaps, we can risk breathing at the edge. But the whalers are out in force to intercept all pods, and they will be listening and watching along the edge of the ice shelf. Besides, we will save many days traveling this way. Even if we could go by open sea, that way is much longer. Our strength would not last the journey."

The pod lay silent, as if stunned.

Finally, Aleea asked, "How do we know there are breathing holes the whole way?"

"We don't," Hrūna responded. "That is why we must send one of us to find them in advance—to scout the way under the ice and return quickly." He looked at me, and all eyes turned. "Hralekana has already agreed to search for a way."

Aleea looked stricken. I turned my face away from her.

"And if he can't find one . . . ?" asked Lewtë, her voice failing.

"If I can't find a way with enough air holes," I said, trying to sound confident, "I will simply head out to the edge of the ice shelf." I had heard stories of how whales, through lack of air, became confused in the perpetual blue twilight under the ice, or how in the pitch dark of night, misled by myriad echoes, they lost all sense of direction.

I knew there was no time to spare, so I said good-bye to the pod, parents, and grandparents, and went aside with Aleea.

"I wish I were going with you," she said, holding back tears.

"Alone I'll travel quickly and be back all the sooner," I said, smiling to reassure her. We pressed against each other. I felt an electric thrill when her side pushed out once, twice, as the new life in it shifted.

"Remember our calf," she said.

"I will," I promised. Then, without looking back, I breathed in deeply and plunged under the glistening white wall. While my eyes adjusted to the cobalt blue light, I heard Aleea's song reach after me:

> Wherever on the waters the winds shall find you,
> Wherever the moon or the sun shall move,
> Hidden in the heavens or splendid high above you,
> Deep in my heart I will breathe deeply with you
> The breath of the one who made you and keeps you.

Her voice trailed off and I was alone.

Chapter Six

I felt a shiver pass down my spine as I looked at the strange and beautiful world before me. The water was absolutely clear and everything in it motionless. Beneath me I could not see bottom, only a deepening blue abyss. Above me a blue light came through the ice, brighter where the ice was thin, darker where it thickened. Growing down from the ceiling hung a network of ice—some in icicles large as the stone ones in Hralekana's cavern, some like coral in crystal branches, and some in a filigree delicate as seaweed. These crystals glinted in the blue light and took fantastic shapes. Gazing up at them, I didn't see a large bunch hanging directly in front of me and swam right into it. I hardly felt it as it broke and scattered around me with a faint ringing music, the pieces flashing like stars into the depths.

Then absolute silence returned. I was enchanted by this empty, silent world and had to remind myself I was on a mission. Every few seconds I let out a series of high-pitched whistles to check my course in this world where every direction looked the same. My plan was to steer a straight course that cut deep under the ice toward where it met the land, yet was still close enough to the outer edge that I could reach the open sea if the breathing holes were closed.

I knew the calves would need to breathe at short intervals, so when not far in I saw a bright patch in the ceiling of ice, I rose up to it. The ice was thin here and I bumped against it. It cracked easily and I pushed through, breathing the fresh, sweet air. I widened the hole, making it easier to find from below and to break through when I returned.

I rested a short while, gazing up at a blue sky and hoping that the pod was hugging the ice pack, staying out of sight of the whalers. Around the hole the ice rose in broken slabs and jagged peaks. I was about to sink under again when I heard a familiar shriek and saw white wings flashing madly through the blue.

It was Ross. He landed, spouting puffs of warm breath, on the edge of a blue slab.

"What's it like under the ice?" he asked, hopping over to my blowhole to tweak it. Knowing the direction I intended to go, he'd guessed my speed and kept watch near this breathing hole.

"It's like your blue sky, only turned upside down," I said. "I feel as if I'm flying—there's nothing under me, and above me the ice grows down like fantastic seaweed and coral."

He sighed and said, "How I wish I could see it!" I laughed and squirted him and he pecked me again. It was a great comfort to see him and speak with him in this solitude, but I had to be off. He promised to continue watching for me.

With that, I sank back into the blue world. Again I checked my course, plotting it as straight as possible. I came to a second hole and a third, but it was getting difficult to see. The blue light thickened. The thin places in the ice ceiling were fading and I knew the sun must be going down, so I aimed at a thin spot and rose to break through it. This one took some doing and I bumped against it with all my weight. With a loud crack, the ice broke and lifted in a slab, which I pushed up over the top.

The sky was a deep purple, and two or three stars had already come out. High up, a dark shape dropped and in a moment Ross was beside me. Tired from the first day, I decided to sleep there.

Ross perched by my blowhole, his head folded under his wing. I fell asleep to the rough music of his snore.

As soon as it was light, I roused Ross. We said good-bye and I slid back under. I had gone a good distance the first afternoon and hoped to go much farther the second day.

Mile after mile, hole after hole, I traveled through the strange blue light, which had the same effect as the silence in Hralekana's cavern. I felt especially alert and still. Once I noticed a flash far below me, followed by a sleek, dark shape. Approaching the next breathing hole, I heard a sharp bark and found the ice already broken. Looking about on the surface, I saw nothing but ice, when suddenly a large reddish head popped up beside me.

"Well, I never. . . " it said, and disappeared. In a second it was back, a large fish in its mouth, which it flipped out on the ice. The head, though large as a walrus's, was that of a seal.

The fat, humorous face stared at me and said, "I've never seen a Humpback or any whale this far under the ice. Are you lost?" It spoke in a breathy manner, as if it had trouble breathing through all the rolls of fat.

Without waiting for a response, it heaved itself onto the ice— a laborious process, or at least not a graceful one. I almost laughed as I watched it flop across to the fish.

"Are you hungry?" it asked, nosing the fish toward me and humping along after it.

"No," I lied politely. The red Weddell seal, for that's what it was, started eating the fish noisily, smacking its lips with relish. When it finished, it belched and looked at me.

"What brings you so far under the ice?"

I explained what brought me there to this large red fellow, grossly fatter than the black seals and sea lions that we usually came across in these waters. A fast and sleek swimmer under the ice, the red seal could swim in farther because of its larger lungs. With its added weight, it could break through the ice to breathe. It hunted the fish that lived under the ice—some without eyes, like fish deep in caves.

The seal, whose name was Gorbov, was intrigued by the story of the pirate whalers and the seal who escaped them—and outraged too at the news of their using nets.

When I told him where I was headed, he described, as best he could, the location of the breathing holes. Between here and the Rock Wall, he said, the holes were fewer and less reliable. When I asked him what he meant by the Rock Wall, he replied, "The great Rock Wall, of course! You haven't passed it before?"

"No," I said. "Usually we swim far out from the ice shelf and do not try to pass to the other side of the Pole."

He explained that the Rock Wall was a tentacle of land that reached far out from the polar ice into the ocean. To go around it meant a journey of many days. I felt my heart sink as he spoke. The other side of the Pole lay beyond this Rock Wall.

I told him of the plight of our pod—how we couldn't take the many days needed to go around the wall nor risk the open water.

He looked troubled on our account and, thoughtfully stroking his whiskers with one flipper, replied, "There is another way, though I have never taken it myself. It is dangerous. Some have lost their wits in it and never seen the light of day again." He shook his head and a shudder moved through all his rolls of fat down to his hind flukes. He paused, staring at the distant ice, caught up in an old memory.

At last, impatient, I asked: "What is that way?"

"Under the water," he replied, "just where the Rock Wall leaves the land, is a cave. It is an endless cave—or, rather, one cave leads to another—and if you swim through the many twists and turns and do not get lost, I am told it opens on the far side of the Rock Wall."

"Is it all underwater?" I asked.

"Yes," Gorbov replied. "But there are breathing spaces near the roof—if you can find them. For one who knows the way and is swift, it is a journey of only one day."

I thanked him for his help, and after breathing deeply for the swim to the next hole, I plunged back into the blue, glowing world under the ice. Far below me I saw the silver glimmer of fish, understanding now why the red seals swam in so far to hunt. Above me the ice was thicker and the light dimmer. There were fewer bright spots, but the same crystals hung down in ever-changing, fascinating shapes.

My sense of finding my way by echo had sharpened, and I knew my course was straight. The distance was farther this time, but the bright space in the ceiling appeared just where Gorbov said it would. I burst through it in a shower of crystals and found Ross waiting for me in sunlight. He'd happened upon the red seal at the last breathing hole and learned that I'd passed by.

Ross looked at me gravely. "Will you try the tunnel?"

I said I had no choice. It was only three breathing holes to the Rock Wall and sundown would bring me there. Since day and night in the tunnel were equally dark, I would go through it this night. Ross nodded silently, clambered onto my back, and rubbed my blowhole with his beak.

We met again at the last three breathing holes but spoke no more of the tunnel. At the third, there was a family of red seals—a mother, father, and pup. They glanced at each other when I mentioned the tunnel. The father, however, agreed to lead me to the entrance. From that last breathing hole I viewed the high mountains that marked the Rock Wall extending beyond sight out to sea. They looked cold, jagged, and forbidding.

Ross paced nervously up and down my spine and made me promise three times to wait at the surface on the far side until he found me.

While we rested, the mother seal asked if I had ever heard the strange tale of the whale who wished to swim under a great land mass. Long ago, when the earth was young, the giant whale had found the deepest cavern on the earth and swam into it, hoping to pass under the land. It was so long and dark that he lost his bearings in it. For centuries, she said, he has wandered there in the dark trying to find his way out. Every now and then one can see his spout rise above a volcano near the shore.

Somehow the story didn't make me feel any better.

Unable to bear seeing me dive, Ross took off toward the mountains. I watched his white shape vanish among the snowy peaks. Then, breathing deeply and with the seal for a guide, I dove under.

The ice was very thick now and the light a deep, luminous blue. After a while we came to the roots of the mountains that made up the Great Rock Wall. The Wall loomed over us darkly, irregular with many bays and coves. At the back of one of these, between two stone roots of the mountain, an enormous blackness opened in the Wall. As we approached, it swelled larger.

At last the seal turned, pointing with his nose. "There it is. Good luck to you!" He turned and streaked west, leaving a trail of silver bubbles.

The longer I gazed at the black opening, the darker it grew. So rather than brood about it, I plunged into the black mouth, uttering short whistles to measure the tunnel's size and shape.

The first part opened into a vast underground cavern. Though I could see nothing but the entrance behind me shrinking to a small blue disk, my ears told me that giant stone teeth hung from the roof and grew from the floor. Toward the rear of the cavern these closed in on one another and the way narrowed. I moved quickly, among a confusing number of echoes. Before I knew it, I ran head-on into a stone tooth. My head exploded with pain and bright lights and my ears rang as the echo of the blow bounced off a thousand surfaces. The stone tooth split my lip and loosened several baleen plates. I lay on the bottom dazed, struggling to retain my air. From then on, I moved more carefully.

The echoes told me there was an outlet at the back of the cave, but to get there I had to squeeze between two stone teeth. When I pushed, I heard a sharp crack, and one of the teeth fell, its stone bulk brushing my side and crashing to the floor. I shuddered at the near miss, fortunate the tooth had not crushed me. I was beginning to need air and anxiously searched the roof for any sign that it rose above the water. There was none.

From the back of the cave I entered a wide tunnel free of the stone teeth. The tunnel slanted down into the bowels of the mountain and fear constricted my throat as I despaired of finding breathing space. Yet I had no choice but to go on. The tunnel angled down, taking several turns, and I lost all sense of direction. Descending, it narrowed and I began to feel closed in.

At last it angled upward under a massive rock that hung so close to the floor I doubted I could pass under it. Yet the tunnel was too narrow for me to turn back. I pressed under the rock and stopped. For a moment I feared I was stuck and would drown there, but calling on all my strength, I squeezed through, scraping my belly and back.

At the top of the next bend I broke through the surface of the water. There was a small breathing space above me, and the air rushed from my lungs. I could just fit my blowhole into it and lay there, puffing in and out until my breathing calmed.

The tunnel twisted down and up again. Then it climbed high inside the mountain, widening on all sides. Soon I came up into a large cavern and once more broke the surface. I saw light. The roof vaulted high above me and the walls receded into shadow. Everything was bathed in a dim light.

Huge waterfalls of stone and white icicles of stone hung from the ceiling far above me. After my eyes adjusted, I saw shapes like walruses and one like a Blue whale, only much larger. Rising over the water were squidlike shapes and monstrous figures of stone like no animal in the sea. The gleaming surface of the pool was perfectly still. Now and then a drop of water landed with a loud *plink* somewhere in the cave and its echo rang back and forth between the walls.

I looked up for the source of the light and saw high above me a shaft of light coming in through a crevice in the mountain wall. With a shock I realized I'd already passed a whole night on this journey. While I gazed, the light slowly brightened to gold. The sun was shining outside. For a moment the cavern brightened and crystals sparkled down the waterfall of stone.

The sun faded, and I swam to the far end of the cavern looking for an outlet. Finding it behind the stone waterfall, I once again descended into the dark.

After hours more of twists and turns and pauses at breathing places, some large, some small, I perceived the tunnel was growing lighter again. Finally I rounded a turn and saw a light in the distance. It was the end of the tunnel on the far side of the Rock Wall.

Outside, I headed immediately to the surface and found no ice blocking it. I breached into a green sea where a fresh gale blew and whitecaps glittered in the sun. Before my eyes could adjust to the light, I heard a familiar shriek and felt a feathery weight land on my back.

"You made it!" Ross cried, breathless. "I knew you would. I've been circling here since dawn." He leaped about my back, performing an awkward flapping dance, pecking at a new barnacle or two for sheer joy.

"It was a tight squeeze at times—and I nearly lost my breath—but you can tell the pod the tunnel's passable."

"For the calves, too?" Ross asked.

"I think so."

The edge of the ice gleamed a mile off, and after resting a while with Ross, I headed for it as he flapped back over the mountains to give the news to the pod. I knew time was running out for them where they waited without food, so now I swam day and night, from breathing hole to breathing hole, and twice I swam out to the edge of the ice where the seal had told me about a deep inlet or bay.

One morning I came out from under the ice to find the sky filled with birds and the sea boiling with seals and whales both large and small. It was a sight I can hardly begin to describe. There, stretching for miles, was the pinkish orange krill, and it was as if all the animals missing from the desolate coast we'd traveled had found their way here. Crowding from the shore were hundreds, even thousands, of icebergs and floes that stretched out for miles from the shelf, affording every kind of shelter to whales, birds, and seals. Penguins by the hundreds leaped from these into the sea, together with the small, comical puffins.

I took one good meal of krill, feeding and resting that whole spring morning.

That afternoon, reluctantly, I turned to go. The return trip went much faster, because I knew the way. I swam without stopping back to the pod.

Chapter Seven

There was much rejoicing when I returned. Aleea rushed to me when I rose from under the blue ice, and the others sang out their greetings, swimming over to crowd about us. I was shocked by how thin they looked and how slowly the old ones moved.

The glad greetings warmed my heart and almost did away with the weariness I felt. I told the story of my journey, lifting their spirits with a description of the krill that awaited them. They reported that the whalers were still blocking the coast, but that the pod had slept undisturbed close to the ice.

That night I slept soundly next to Aleea at the center of the pod, all of us too tired for any further celebration. In the thick fog before sunrise, Aleea nudged me awake. She motioned to me to be quiet and listen.

For a moment I didn't hear anything. Then I heard it—*wiss wiss wiss*—the quiet turning of something through the water. The fog was growing lighter as the sun prepared to rise, but we could see nothing nor hear any of the usual sounds from the insides of ships.

Wiss wiss wiss—something was coming toward us so quietly I thought it might be one of the iron whales I had met in the other ocean. I was still trying to identify the noise when three dark blurs appeared through the fog.

They were whalers all right, and they were right on top of us. They'd moved in silently, in the darkness and fog. Now they roared into life. *Thrug thrug thrug*, they lurched toward us, only a few whale-lengths away. *Ping* came the sharp echo finders—*Ping*.

"Swim for your life!" we shouted to the pod, waking mothers and calves and pushing them toward the ice. The whales breathed in once, twice, and lobtailed. One mother was having trouble with her calf. Coming up on either side of it, Aleea and I pressed it firmly between us and dove.

In a moment everyone was under the ice. I cried for them to follow me. With Hrūna, Lewtë, and Aleea bringing up the stragglers, I led them into that cobalt blue world.

I knew we could not go in far. Some had taken the merest gulp of air before diving. At the first thin place in the blue ceiling, I rose up and broke through the ice. The other adults followed, and in a short time we made a large breathing hole filled with icy fragments. The calves surfaced last, sputtering and gasping, and lay there catching their breath. We did nothing but breathe for a long time.

"We'll rest here until everyone has enough air," I said. They all turned toward me. "From now on when we travel, there will be one grown-up with every yearling and two with every calf." I stared hard at the calves. "There will be no needless talk or movement. From here on, breathing holes are few and far between." I gave other instructions and we rested there while the morning sky brightened from deep pink to blue.

The world under the ice was beautiful now, and despite their fear, I saw wonder fill the eyes of the others. The crystals, hanging everywhere in splendid profusion, intrigued all. There was a tinkling sound, and two calves shot by me through the suspended crystals, sending them flashing and ringing to the Deep. The two squealed with delight and two more, Hrēta and the yearling Hronto, shot ahead and wreaked musical havoc among the crystals.

"Stop them!" I cried out, sorry to spoil the fun. Still, there was a whole symphony of crystal-breaking before everyone was back in line.

"You'll need all your breath to reach the next hole," I warned the calves, trying hard to keep a straight face. Despite the seriousness of wasting breath, the music and play had cheered up the pod, and now and then an adult brushed against the crystals to hear them ring out through the Deep.

The pod formed a line behind me: the calves in front, each flanked by two adults, followed by the yearlings, the old ones, and last, those in their prime. There was little noise as we swam, the ever-changing crystals sparkling above us and the blue glow descending to infinity.

We were no more than halfway to the next breathing hole when the two smallest calves complained they needed air. We told them to hold on, but a few minutes later they complained again and we saw by their faces they needed it fast. One was swimming crookedly.

I signaled to the parents and swiftly they lifted both calves to the ice ceiling between the hanging crystals. There were recesses in the uneven ice and into one of these the parents breathed some of their precious air, making a pocket for the calves to breathe. As a precaution, the other parents did the same.

We made the next breathing hole without further incident. Ali, Ala, and Ross were waiting for us and greeted everyone with glad cries. On the ice rested the same family of red Weddell seals I had met closer to the Rock Wall. The seal pup frisked about with some of the calves, teasing them and clambering out over the ice when they chased him. Once he waddled menacingly toward Ross, who squawked and flapped his wings in mock terror.

Quietly, so as not to alarm the others, the father seal told me breathing holes ahead of us were harder to open now, due to a freeze at night. I kept the news to myself but hurried the others on.

That night we lay side by side, crowded in a breathing hole, the stars above us large as gulls and their reflections glistening off the wet backs of the whales. The three albatrosses slept on our heads, familiar silhouettes against the stars. I couldn't sleep, worried as I was about the slow pace of the pod. It would take us twice the time it took me to make this under-ice journey. After a while the beauty of the stars comforted me, and I lay awake watching the Leaping Whale finish his enormous jump across the sky.

Over the next few days we drew near to the Rock Wall. Two breathing holes away from it, the ice was too thick to break. We tried our best, and several of us bruised ourselves badly, throwing all our weight against the ice. That was a bad moment. Hard up for air ourselves, we had to give air a second or even third time to the calves. I decided our only chance was to swim to the edge of the ice shelf and risk having the whalers find us. It was a shorter distance to open water than to the next breathing hole, which might also be frozen solid.

At a word, the pod followed me. That was a difficult time. Three of the calves grew dizzy and had to be carried by their parents, which slowed everyone. When at last we reached open water, no iron monsters were to be seen—nor were our friends the albatrosses, who did not know we'd changed course.

The calves and grown-ups gulped air, but one new calf, Hrassa, floated motionless and failed to breathe. His eyes were shut and his blowhole sealed tight. His parents cried out in fear and rubbed him briskly on both sides. I joined them and pushed him high out of the water, letting him drop to the surface with a slap. At that, his flukes twitched slightly, and after more pounding and slapping, he choked, spouted water, and gasped. We were overjoyed.

We rested there for the night and the next day two strong swimmers scouted ahead to be sure the last breathing hole before the Rock Wall was open. There they found three desperately worried albatrosses who, failing to meet us at the frozen breathing hole, thought we had all drowned.

Later the pod arrived, and again we rested the entire night while I carefully explained to the others every twist and turn and breathing space in the tunnel. Once again, Ross slept by my blowhole, snoring softly.

In the morning we descended to the dark roots of the mountains and entered the shadowy mouth of the passage. We went through the first cave easily, but soon we were crowded in the tunnel and had to take turns breathing from the small pockets of air. The whole day passed before we reached the giant cavern with the stone waterfalls. When we did, it was pitch dark. Exhausted, we spread out on the surface, breathing freely. We rested till dawn when the light coming in showed the dim outlines of the strange and beautiful stones.

We lay there silent, in awe of the majestic shapes above us. Then the calves, who'd been afraid of the darkness and silence, revived, and discovered the echo in the huge cavern. They squealed until I feared the roof would fall from the sound bouncing off every stone tooth and reverberating from every bay and chamber behind the stone waterfalls and crystal reefs.

At one point I heard something crack and a small stone tooth fell from the ceiling, narrowly missing a calf. I called for silence and hurried everyone out the far end. We had not gone very far down the tunnel when we heard the thunder of rocks falling. The water surged behind us, and when we reached the place where the next breathing space should be, the water had risen and filled it. Six of us gave up air to make a pocket for the calves to breathe.

When we arrived at the next breathing space, two of the older whales, Hrobo and Hreena, were too weak to go on. I told the others to go ahead without us. They were near the end of the tunnel and would reach it easily. I stayed with the exhausted elders while they rested before swimming feebly toward the tunnel mouth.

When we at last came out into the light, the pod was waiting. In daylight it was clear that starvation was taking its toll. The bones showed through the faces and sides of many, and all lay listlessly on the surface. We spoke very little. After resting a half day, I led them, reluctantly, back under the ice.

The last part of the journey was a long blue nightmare of feeble motion, hunger pangs, and calves who had to be carried. It became increasingly harder to break through the ice over the breathing holes. Fortunately, the albatrosses scouted these for us and told us in advance of their condition. Several times we had to swim for the edge of the ice shelf because of a solidly frozen hole, wasting precious time and energy.

At last we were only one day's swim from the krill beds. But I knew we had barely enough strength to get there. If we did not make it that day, many would perish. The calves could scarcely move and had to be carried. While I lay awake worrying that night, I saw a drop of spray from the Leaping Whale's flukes flash across the sky in the direction of the krill. I took hope from it and was finally able to sleep.

The next morning, pounding at the ice over the last breathing hole, we were too weak to break through. It was ironic, I thought, to perish a short way from the open sea and food. I battered my head once more against the ice, with no luck. I was growing dizzy and thought how stupid I'd been to bring the weakened pod under the ice a second time.

I sank, determined to throw myself against the ice once more, though I die. Then I saw a shadow in the corner of one eye, and I thought my sight was fading. But the shadow moved, and I realized it was a bird flapping on top of the ice in a different place from where we were trying to break through. "Ross," I thought. "Ross is showing us the right spot."

Giddy from lack of air, I threw myself toward his shadow. The ice burst with a sharp crack, and I was out in the sunlight.

Crack, crack, crack, the others widened the hole around me and with a glad squawk Ross landed on my nose. In a minute everyone was out, the calves having to be held up while they breathed.

In the distance we heard the cry of birds and the bark of seals, and then a breeze moved from the east and we all smelled it—the rich sea smell of the krill beds. Some broke into snatches of song, their voices weak. From the eyes of others ran tears. Even the calves paddled weakly about the breathing hole.

"It's not far from here," I croaked in a whisper and sank into the blue for the last part of our journey. We paused twice to give air to the calves before the brightening water revealed the edge of the ice.

At last we rose in the open and looked out upon a living world of birds, seals, and penguins, as well as the oddly shaped spouts of Fin, Sei, and Blue whales. Behind and among them the ice mountains floated and sang their harsh music. And all about them, as far as the eye could see, floated the pink krill, stretching to a sky flushed with the dawn.

Chapter Eight

For a long while the members of the pod lay there by the edge of the ice, catching their breath, checking scratches and bruises and examining the calves. These last came alive at the sight of open water, squealing and wriggling about. But some of the elders could scarcely move.

A breeze brought the rich smell of krill full into our faces, and we slowly sculled across the bright reach of water separating us from it. Cries of gulls and curlews dropped about us like rain in the fresh dawn as the Red Bull of the Sun raised his head above the horizon, his fiery track leading to the krill. Far off we saw the spouts of whales deep in the krill and heard them trumpet, sigh, and lobtail as they fed. The icebergs sang and howled and turned in various lights, rainbows forming among them in the mist. It was a fine spring morning. The cold snap had passed.

The calves were begging to feed and it did the heart good to see shining eyes and eager smiles on those pinched, thin faces. We cautioned them to eat slowly, for their stomachs needed to adjust to so much food.

With trumpets of joy, the mothers plunged into the wall of krill before us, making large holes through which their calves followed. The rest of the pod followed after, leaving the albatrosses to keep watch.

In less than an hour, most had returned to the edge to rest and to digest the krill. Throughout that day by turns we nibbled and rested. Everyone's color revived, and those who had barely kept going under the ice now leaped and swam vigorously. Aleea, though thin, looked sleek and bright-eyed.

The mothers' milk had come back after drying up on our journey, and the calves—still weaning—fed long into that moonlit night. The milk that missed their mouths bubbled and churned under the moon.

We were all tired, now that the pangs of hunger had been stilled. But before we settled down to sleep, in gratitude for our safe journey, we sang the Song of the Krill, followed by the Song of the Dark Passage, composed that very day by Hrobo between courses of krill:

> White rose the ice, to the eye wild,
> Where it groaned and crumbled to the grim sea.
> Thick was the fog when the foe fell upon us
> And we fluked and fled far under the ice
> To the blue world of the hanging crystals,
> Where the ceiling of ice sealed off air
> And we pooled our breath to keep the calves breathing.
> O what music we made as we crashed through the crystals,
> Sending them flashing far into the Deep!
> How we battered and banged heads hard on the ice
> To break our way through to bright air overhead!
> But darker still than the Blue Deep we dared
> Was the tunnel that pierced the heart of the mountain,
> The caves deep and quiet where we crowded together
> Seeking pockets of air as we pushed through the blackness,
> Then up to the cavern with the crystal fall of water—
> Long teeth taunting us from the mouth of the mountain.
> These closed behind us with thunder and crashing

When we fled down the tunnel again into blackness
That at last opened out to the dazzle of ocean.
There we wandered under ice though our strength was waning,
Famished we followed the most fearless of leaders,
Till we came where the krill swam in sweetest of waters.

Then from overhead, we heard a string of high, eerie notes in patterns strange to us. The albatrosses were responding to Hrobo's Song of the Dark Passage with one of their own about their flight over the top of the ice:

Floating slowly over the high white mountains,
Blue forever above us, white forever below,
On the cold blast blowing from the end of the earth,
Anxious, we searched for the black pools below us
Where friends under ice could breathe the fresh air.
Through dazzling sun by day, cold moon by night,
We glided on the breath of the glacier beneath us,
Following our friends while they fared under ice
To where rainbows glimmered at the rim of the world.

Afterward we rocked to sleep under the moon. Against her bright disk we saw the silhouettes of the albatrosses floating and keeping watch.

The next day the feasting began at dawn and went on to nightfall. We buried ourselves in the fresh krill, swimming with mouths wide, straining out ton after ton. The calves and mothers swelled visibly that day. Bones no longer protruded and slack skin filled out. The calves played hide-and-seek with each other down the tunnels and wide swaths in the krill cut by grown-ups. These were constantly closing and shifting behind them, which made it a fascinating game, when they weren't too busy eating to play.

In the middle of the krill I saw something yellow flash and I surfaced. In a moment an enormous blue back rose up through the krill and spouted.

"Bala!" I cried out, for indeed it was he—Bala the Blue whale whom I met long ago toward the other end of the world.

When he recognized me he called out my name and rolled in delight, showing alternately his sunrise yellow belly and blue back. We bumped and touched flippers. A second enormous belly rolled up beside him.

"Well, I'll be a wrinkled cod—" I started, and fell speechless at the sight of another Blue as large as Bala.

"Hralekana, this is Belah," Bala said.

She smiled a long blue smile, and I called out to Aleea to join us. The four of us spent the rest of the day feeding side by side and telling about the past several years. Bala recounted his meeting with Belah and said both of them had come across very few other Blue whales. Belah also had been alone from the time her parents were killed by pirate whalers. They had met at these krill beds, which, though vast, were crowded with animals fleeing from the oil spill on the far side of the Pole.

Belah and Bala had become mates and she, like Aleea, was with calf. The two females swam off together, deep in talk.

That was a happy time of reunion. The members of the pod met old friends in the krill and among the ice mountains—Seis, Fins, Minkes, dolphins, and large pods of seals, including my grandfather's friend Siloa, nearly all gray now, and blind in one eye. His numerous offspring played with our calves until they were unbearably giddy and exhausted. I even met two sea gulls who said I had saved their lives years before, carrying them out of an oil spill.

Far out in the bay one day I heard the sharp cries of Uton and his pack of Killer whales, and I called out to them. They swam up, as sleek and swift as ever, and we shared a good laugh over their frightening me as a calf—though even now the memory sent a chill through me.

One day, while swimming in the dark emerald waters under an ice mountain, I turned a corner of ice and nearly bumped into a Green turtle. We both backpaddled and looked at each other. Sea moss grew from the ridges of his shell.

I had never seen a turtle so large. He was obviously an old-timer. He blinked heavy-lidded eyes at me and stared.

"Well, flip me over and call me a clam!" he exclaimed. "These old eyes are deceiving me. Hralekana, is that really you? I had heard you were dead."

I'd never seen him before. Puzzled, I replied, "I am the second Hralekana—Hralekana-kolua. Perhaps you mistake me for my namesake, Hralekana the First, of glorious memory."

"Wait . . ." he moved closer. "Yes . . . yes . . ." he said, his eyes clouding over while he slowly waved his flippers, floating in place. "That's right, I *had* heard that Hralekana died fighting the iron monsters." He paused a moment.

"You look just like him—a white Humpback much larger than a Humpback ought to be," he murmured dreamily, then cleared his throat and snapped fully awake. "But, here," he said, turning, "follow me back among the ice, away from these noisy shrimp strainers and loudmouthed seals. I was just headed back there for some quiet. Come and tell me about your travels."

Curious as to what he knew of the first Hralekana, I followed him back to a green lagoon in the ice, surrounded by tall, white walls. We floated there while I told him about myself and my travels.

Now and then Torvald, as he was called, would nod, as if what I told him agreed with something he already knew. He'd heard of the iron whales that swam under the sea, of the great iron monster that struck an iceberg, and of the last season's oil spill. He'd even heard of the *Rainbow Whale* and her pursuit of the ships that carried the deadly fire to eat an island.

Then it was my turn to question, and I asked about Hralekana the First.

The Green turtle gazed far off, as if peering into the depths of time. "I knew of him long ago when I was no bigger than my flipper here and Hralekana, together with a Sperm whale and a Blue, was battling the wooden monsters. When I was grown, I went to visit him in his cavern beneath the ocean and he told me much of the sad history of whales and men, and the history of the whole world.

"From that time on, I was eager to learn all I could of the world, its history, and what was in it. And indeed I have heard many strange and marvelous things."

"Have you heard," I asked, "of the sea people, of the mermen and mermaids? I have heard their music at a distance, and once I thought I glimpsed one. But a friend of mine has actually seen them and heard them sing close by."

"Ah, the sea people!" Torvald said, and closed his eyes. The sun was overhead and shining down warmly in our ice valley, and I thought Torvald might have drifted off to sleep. I cleared my throat and his eyes opened.

"The sea people . . . What I have to tell you now may sound very strange, but it is true. It happened so long ago that no one living can count the years.

"Thousands and thousands of years ago there was a large island in the ocean on the far side of the world—closer to the other

Pole. This island was larger than any island I can think of, yet not so large as one of the great land masses. On that island lived the sea people. In shape they were most like humans from the land, but they loved the ocean as much as those of us born in it. They had flukes like those of us in the sea as well as the clever flippers of humans, which could make many things.

"They loved the creatures of the sea, and many thousands lived around that island and swam, spoke, and sang with the sea people. They invited large numbers of your ancestors to sing in chorus with them on the night of a full moon, together with seals, sea lions, and birds. We turtles swam there by the hundreds, just to listen.

"Then one night a star fell from the sky and struck the ocean. It was so large, a giant wave came and covered the home of the sea people, and they were swept out into the main ocean. Many drowned. When the tidal wave had passed, the ocean level was higher, and all their island was covered by water. The sea people who survived gathered in small groups and swam to the far ends of the earth to find shelter on smaller islands.

"Up until after the time I was born, they were seen frequently. But as humans from the shore sailed farther and farther out, as wooden monsters, and then iron, became plentiful, the mermen and mermaids hid themselves more and more carefully, knowing that the men from land would kill or capture them and force them to live in captivity."

"Have you ever seen them?" I asked.

He said nothing, but his eyes filled with a faraway look.

"Once," he said. "Once when I was new to the ocean, a great typhoon drove me deep into the water where I hoped to escape the violence of the waves and the sharp thrusts of Ohobo's fiery harpoon. As I approached the bottom, I was caught in a sudden current so swift I couldn't swim against it. In fact, I couldn't swim at all but was swept along tail over nose into the Black Deep.

"For a while I thought I would drown, but then my need for air eased and the cold current moved more slowly. Finally right side up, I floated along in it until at last it bent upward and the water shone lighter. It grew warmer, too, and I saw the sun winkling and frazzling on the surface. In a moment the current swept me to the top and the waves rolled green and white about me. The water was pleasantly cool and the air warm and filled with a fine fragrance. The sun was burning through a haze of clouds and the whole sky had a golden tint.

"I looked about and saw I was close to an island made of a single mountain that rose straight out of the sea. The rocky cliffs were washed in the gold mist. In a deep cleft between the cliffs curled a small beach and I swam toward it. Weary, I crawled half up on the strip of golden sand to soak in the warmth of the sun.

"It was then that I heard the music." He paused and his voice trembled. "It seemed to come right out of the rock and encircle me. I can't describe this music, except to say it was the most beautiful I've ever heard. It filled me and seemed to vibrate from my shell and from my bones. The voices in it were new to me. I looked around for the source but saw nothing but rock.

"Then I looked back toward the water and saw seven faces just above the surface, faces I had never seen the likes of but later came to know as human faces. They appeared to be trailing seaweed at first, but when they rose from the water, I saw it was long fur that hung from their heads. They had long flippers and smooth skin down to the middle, but beyond that they were formed to swim in the sea. What struck me most, beside their voices, were their eyes, which were large and bright and piercingly green."

He stopped and stared, as if seeing them before him now.

"They came in a circle around me. I was afraid at first, though enchanted by their voices. They circled me, singing, and then all seven lifted me up with their beautiful flippers, their faces close about me. As they sang, their voices flooded my shell. They filled me with an intense light, and an intense desire. I somehow knew that . . . " His voice failed, and he looked down before continuing.

"I think I grew faint, for their faces disappeared in the light. I must have swooned because I remember nothing more until I woke in the dark, cold current that swept me along as before. But I did hear a long trailing snatch of their song, distant and fading, until it vanished in the rush of the waters.

"The current returned me to my usual haunts. The storm had passed and the sun was out when I paddled weakly to the surface. I told no one where I had been and spent the next days in silence thinking about what I had seen. I was filled with a strong desire that seemed to have no object. At night under the moon I watched the whitecaps play, tossing their foamy crests like the long hair of the mermen, and now and then catching what I thought was a whisper of their distant music.

"After a while I didn't think of them as often and was caught up in the ordinary duties and pleasures of life. But at odd moments the thought of the sea people would return, especially when I found something beautiful. Then I'd be pierced again by a pang of desire. Or when I saw something new and marvelous or touched with mystery. Often ordinary things, too, would bring them to mind—a bit of foam flying or sunlight flashing from a wave."

When he finished, he rolled over on his back, exposing his plated belly to the sun, and stretched his neck out, waggling his flippers. We both were silent a long time.

"Meeting them was almost my undoing," Torvald said finally, his eyes still closed. "When I first came across human creatures in a boat, I thought by their faces they were mermen, and I swam up to them. They reached out and lifted me into the boat. But they didn't sing. Instead they bound my jaws and feet together with a cruel snakelike weed. They made harsh sounds and faces, and poked and prodded me with sticks while the wind carried us along.

"At the shore, they thrust me into a dark cave with a net across the front, but I managed to scrape the weed off my jaws and chewed through the net. Another turtle in there—a Hawk-jaw—smaller than I, escaped with me. Ever since, I have kept my distance from humans."

I told Torvald how I also was once trapped by humans. He was fascinated to learn how Mark and I became friends and that the two of us spoke with each other.

He nodded sagely when I told him that Mark and I shared pictures in our heads even though we didn't understand many of each other's words.

"It's as I thought," he said. "All creatures' minds touch one another. And words, however good, cannot show all that goes on in the head and heart."

We lingered there in the ice that afternoon while Torvald told me many another curious tale, including one of a human calf swept over the side of a boat and how he saved his life. The human calf clung to Torvald's shell while he swam, tirelessly following the boat to an island. When he crawled ashore, a large crowd of grown-ups ran toward them, crying out to the water-soaked child, but Torvald did not wait for their thanks. He scrambled back into the water as fast as he could.

In return, I told him the story of how I rescued the sailor who'd fallen overboard trying to hook me. At that, he opened his mouth and gave off a long series of wheezes from the depths of his shell. I thought he was choking until it dawned on me the wheezes were his turtle laugh.

He was curious about my singing and whether I'd composed any songs of my own. To answer him, I sang a song I made up on the spot about his story of the sunken land. It enchanted him and he begged to hear it a second time:

> Long years ago when the young light came leaping
> Over the waves that blew wild and white,
> In the middle of Ocean lay the mountain of mermen,
> Fair island that idled in the musical air.
> There whale and merman sang blithely together,
> Dancing in the Deep till the waves danced with them
> In the gold light of evening that lingered till midnight.
>
> Then a star fell from heaven in the wrath of a storm,
> Crashed in the ocean while the red lightning roared—
> Ohobo's harpoon struck the walls of the world,
> And a fearful wave rose from the floor of the ocean,
> Lifted up hoary head higher than the mountains.
> Its high black wall in the night heaved passing
> Fathoms over the land where the sea people lay
> And swept them out to sea, to the world's far corners.
>
> Roaring, the wave climbed up all the coastline,
> Flooding the caves far in from the seashore.
> Green and deep it rests over the mermen's island.
> Now fish swim above the land's highest mountain,

Sunlight wavers watery over empty dwellings,
And only silence sings of the people who swam there.

Afterward, Torvald was silent, and a tear slid down his old, leathery face. He pulled his head inside his shell and spoke in a voice cavelike and hollow: "Your song moves me. Only one other have I heard that moved me more, and that was the song of the sea people themselves when they lifted me up and sang through every crevice in my green shell till it vibrated like a conch pressed to their lips."

When he said that, it reminded me of a song one of the greatest of Humpback singers sang long ago about the sea people and their lost island:

> *. . . Great Whales! I'd rather be*
> *A porpoise flung there by some wild storm,*
> *So might I, swimming in that pleasant lea,*
> *Have visions that would leave me less forlorn:*
> *Have sight of mermaids rising from the sea*
> *Or hear old Triton blow his wreathéd horn.*

Triton was the legendary leader of the sea people who warned them the night of the tidal wave by blowing on a conch shell, a shell from which he drew incomparable music. Legend has it that after the remnant of mermen were scattered to the seven seas, he caused islands to rise from the ocean floor by playing his magical conch—islands honeycombed with sea caves lit by the sun—where the sea people could ever after take shelter.

That night I introduced Torvald to the rest of the pod, and calf and grown-up alike, we stayed up listening to his stories and sharing our own. One by one the calves, the mothers, and even Old Hrobo himself drifted off to sleep before Torvald had finished. Still, there were four or five of us who spoke with him into the early hours until the Leaping Whale's spray of stars faded into the dawn.

Chapter Nine

Over the remaining weeks at the krill beds, the pod made friends with the other baleen whales—all of us "shrimp strainers," as my friend Spygga the Sperm whale called us, sharing the delicacy krill as our favorite food. Besides Bala the Blue and his mate Belah, we made friends with Fin whales and Sei and a Right whale or two.

It was wonderful to get to know so many other whales, yet all of us were aware that it was the destruction of the krill on the far side of the Pole that brought us to these beds, now slowly shrinking from the presence of too many feeders. Still, it was a joy to watch the others grow fat and sleek. Aleea was almost too busy eating to talk, and she swelled doubly fast as the calf inside her grew.

At night we sang and told stories and even celebrated three glorias on the nights of three full moons, before the onset of colder weather warned us it was time to begin the journey home to the tropical islands of our birth. We were told by both dolphins and the albatrosses, who had flown for two days scouting the coast, that the whaling fleet had ended their season early and were far out in the ocean, steaming away from the Pole.

Still, we waited for a week after we heard that news and, carefully hugging the ice, began the journey back to the other side of the Pole. We knew the way we chose was long, yet considerably easier than traveling under the ice. We went slowly, leisurely, on the surface, the calves romping and chasing each other in our wake. What a difference in mood there was from that of the starved and silent figures on the journey over.

The weather was clear and the sun bright, though the nights were colder. This cheered our spirits, but worried me. No clouds in the sky meant that we were easier to spot by the enemy—by any iron bird or thunderwing that flew over. But I said nothing to the pod.

After a few days we came again to the Rock Wall, the range of mountains that thrust out from the ice of the Pole far into the ocean. The icy peaks were beautiful to behold against the blue sky, but no ice pack clung to those sheer cliffs and we would be exposed for days as we swam around them.

Fortunately, Torvald had told me of three underwater caverns in the Rock Wall that might provide refuge from danger. But the distances between them were long. Our best plan if attacked was to hug the Rock Wall itself and hope any whaling ship feared sailing too close to the rocks.

With all these thoughts troubling me, I kept up an appearance of calm and good cheer when the pod left the protection of the ice to travel along that barren coast. Most were filled with curiosity and excitement. The albatrosses flew above us and a pod of dolphins swam and leaped to starboard, carrying on a high-pitched conversation with the calves, who frisked with them in high spirits.

For two days we traveled away from the ice along the Rock Wall, and the good weather stayed with us. I was increasingly uneasy the farther we ventured from the ice and at times regretted not having tried to pass back through the tunnel. The elders of the Council shared my concern, but we hid our anxiety from the rest, who were in a merry mood.

On the third day the sun still shone but was overcast with mist, a white blur burning in a white sky. The mist added to my uneasiness as we passed and left behind the first of the underwater caves. Still, the albatrosses reported nothing. Apparently we had the sea to ourselves.

Late on the third day, while the sun sank in a band of swollen purple clouds, we rounded the end of the Rock Wall and started back on the other side. My spirits rose slightly, since we were now swimming toward the ice, however distant. The maroon glow of the setting sun stained the waters west of us.

That night we slept near the mouth of the second cave. Aleea and I dove under to explore it. We found the opening narrow and hard to squeeze through. Inside, our echoes told us the cave was not large—barely big enough to hold the pod. Worse, it narrowed toward the top. There was room for only two adults to breathe at one time. The air was stale from little exchange with the outside. It would do in an emergency, however, and the pod went to sleep near the cave's mouth, feeling secure.

I was beginning to worry less, and Aleea helped.

"The mist has filled your brain," she said. "You hardly speak."

"You're right," I confessed. "I've been in cold seas too long." I nuzzled her swollen sides. She fled and I chased after her. In a small cove of the cliff we rolled, and again I felt the calf inside her move.

"Aha!" I said, drawing back. "That one has swallowed his share of krill." Aleea laughed and ducked and fled from me again. Later, we swam slowly back to the pod, speaking of times to come.

The next day we woke in fog and guided ourselves along the cliffs more by sound than sight. The albatrosses hung close, three black blurs in the fog, which was motionless, thick, and wet.

Now and then one gave out a cry that sounded muted and weird in that fog. Around noon the fog lifted and we glimpsed the ghost of a sun above us, shrouded in mist. Luckily we found a school of herring near the shore and cheered ourselves with a savory meal.

It grew dark early that night, and we stopped not far from the third and last of the underwater refuges. It was too late to explore the cave, and we lapsed into an uneasy sleep.

Something woke me early. I didn't know what. All was silent except for the steady breathing of the whales and an occasional mutter from our friends on the cliff above, where Ross talked in his sleep. I listened long but heard nothing unusual and was just about to drift back to sleep when a muffled sound came through the dark—no doubt the same that woke me. It was very faint, a soft thud followed by a slight ringing, as if one heavy piece of metal struck another. And it was close by.

Afraid to make any noise, I nudged Aleea awake and the two of us woke the others. We lay there alert while the fog grew lighter. Dawn was coming. We heard the sound once again, and this time it was closer still. Quietly we edged toward the Rock Wall, swimming along it in the direction of the cave. The mountains now separated themselves from the fog, looming as dark shadows on our left.

We traveled closer to the cave when another shadow appeared ahead, on our right, then another. The pod stopped, alarmed, and several of us moved forward for a better look. A morning breeze blew from the mountaintops and parted the fog. There, less than half a mile away, between us and the cave, lay two iron monsters—two whalers with their lights out. I saw the white faces of men along the top and one standing behind each harpoon.

Quickly we submerged, hoping we'd not been seen. But just as we did, *ping ping ping*, the echo finders started and with a clang and rumble so did the ships' engines. Up through the water we saw flashes on the surface as the eyes of each ship lit up. There were bangs and clanks and the light scuffle of hundreds of humans moving inside the whalers' bellies. We'd been spotted and they were bearing down on us.

"Quick!" I shouted. "Dive deep and swim as close as you can to the Rock Wall." In the dark water we heard ship after ship start its engines. It sounded as if the entire whaling fleet had spent the night on this side of the Rock Wall. I rose to find many ships' eyes, red and green, closing on us. As soon as I broke water, a wet, frantic Ross settled on my nose.

"There are dozens," he said, "including three large mother ships that swallow whales whole. Half are on this side of the Rock Wall and half on the other side chasing Fins and Seis."

"Where did they come from?" I asked.

"They are the same ones we saw steaming away from the Pole." Ross nearly toppled into the water, bending over to stare into my eye. "They must have turned around in the fog and come back here to wait."

I dove to tell the others. Everyone swam close to the cliffs: first the calves and the mothers, with the rest to the outside. The catchers in front of us headed into the wall, as close as they dared, to cut us off. Behind us and alongside pressed others, looking for stragglers. Beyond them, blurs of light marked the rest of the fleet.

The fog thinned. Beyond the catchers I saw the ghostly outline of a huge factory ship—white, studded with a thousand eyes.

Hugging the Wall, we approached the first catcher, which had nosed in to the cliffs. With its prow curved back like the jaw of a shark, it rumbled hungrily, stirring up foam as it churned in one place. I rose to spyhop. I hoped the sight of me would distract the harpooner. But the ship stayed in position while he crouched behind the gleaming harpoon, staring at the small stretch between him and the cliffs.

I threw myself up and out of the water as a decoy while the others swam toward that lethal nose. Men ran back and forth along the rail, shouting and pointing at me. The harpooner looked my way and started to swing the harpoon, but the ship stayed where it was. By now the calves and mothers were passing underwater by the ship's nose. Lobtailing with a loud slap, I plunged and brought up the rear.

The moment I passed the ship, its engines roared into life. We were still a distance from the cave mouth. Meanwhile, two more catchers came up behind the first one. Worse, the fog was gone and the sky clearing; I could see blue patches through the surface. The whole ocean thrummed and vibrated with the sounds from the whaling fleet. And the calves needed to come up for breath before they reached the mouth of the cave.

We were halfway to the cave when I heard a familiar chopping sound. Looking up, I saw a thunderwing hovering in the air directly over us. I wondered what it was going to do, when a small bundle of red sticks fell out of it, splashed on the surface, and sank toward the bottom.

Suddenly there was a flash and a roar in the deep and the water squeezed unbearably about me and the others, almost forcing out our breath. It hurt our ears and the pod panicked, rushing toward the surface.

"No!" I cried. "Don't go up. They want that. They'll kill you." The pod leveled off, but several cried out. Two of the calves were bleeding from their blowholes. Aleea's cousin Hrēta was dazed, swimming on her side. Aleea helped the mother carry Hrēta along. Other adults, seeing the calves move slowly, came up beside them. Two would press a calf between them, carrying it swiftly under the catcher.

Two calves popped to the surface by the side of the whaler. Their parents rushed after them. Old Hrobo also lurched up right under the catcher's bow. Blood was trickling from his mouth and he waggled his flippers weakly. I came up under him and pushed. An instant later I heard the sharp roar of a harpoon and bright steel streaked over him, narrowly missing his hump and shattering in an explosion and shower of sparks against the Rock Wall.

I pushed Hrobo along and for a minute the catcher couldn't follow, reeling in the long snake to which the harpoon was attached.

"Breathe!" I cried to the pod, and they did, for a few seconds. By then Hrobo had recovered a bit and dove after me. Hrunta and I closed in on either side to help him along.

"Let go of me," he said in a whisper, "and save yourselves. I am old. I have seen my day." But we ignored his words. Slowed down by his weight, we watched the others vanish in the distance. The three catchers shadowed us while we swam, waiting for us to breach again.

By the time we reached the underwater cave's entrance, all the others were inside. Besides the three that followed us, there were two more catchers waiting opposite its mouth.

Bubble by bubble, Hrobo was releasing his air, and I knew we had only a few seconds. Pushing with all our might, we squeezed him through the entrance and struggled to bring him up to the air at the top. It was pitch black, and the pod was crowded at the surface but dropped back at our cries to make way for Hrobo.

At the top he did not breathe, and we feared the worst. But the pod took turns pummeling him and lifting him above the surface, and after a minute or two water erupted from his blowhole and he inhaled a long, raspy breath. He opened his eyes and blinked.

"I saw my whole life swim before me," he said in a low whisper, "and I saw the most beautiful light. . . . Then you pushed the water from my lungs." His voice in that dark place had a faraway sound to it.

Torvald's knowledge of these caves had saved our lives. We were safe, for the moment, but we were also trapped. We knew that the whalers could wait for us to come out and from here it was a long swim, at least a day's, to the polar ice on this side of the Rock Wall.

In the dark we attended to the air-starved calves and to Hrobo. There was no light, but echoes told us a lot about our condition—even what might be injured inside. Many anxious moments were spent as mother and father carefully examined their calves. Fortunately, the explosion from the thunderwing had been a small one, and what we found were only bloody blowholes and, at worst, a damaged eardrum. What had slowed the calves and made them swim erratically was lack of air.

It was harder to tell with old Hrobo, who had many ailments associated with his years. But he seemed to be gaining strength.

In that dark place, with the presence of everyone close around us offering comfort, the Council spoke long about what we should do.

"It's clear," Hrūna said, "that if we all go out together in day-light, it won't be long before we have to surface and they will kill us." There was a groan from the pod as this truth sank in.

"What are we to do then?" asked Hrekka.

The Council spoke long and earnestly about various plans. There was much discussion of what we should do, but finally, re-luctantly, we agreed upon a course of action that no one liked very much but seemed the only one possible.

The plan decided upon was this: We would wait in the cave until night. Then by ones or—in the case of a calf and its mother—twos, we would leave the cave and hug the Rock Wall, moving as quietly as possible underwater toward the Polar ice.

Hrekka would go out first to scout and make contact with Ala and family. After he reported it was safe, the calves and mothers would leave, and last, the other grown-ups, with myself bringing up the rear. Members of the Council would swim at intervals among the others, ready to rise and act as decoys, if necessary, to lead the catchers away from the Wall. If we were lucky, the dawn would find us within sight of the ice shelf.

We settled down as much as possible for some sleep, the calves floating at the top by the air pocket. The adults took turns rising among them for air.

Chapter Ten

The dim light at the entrance to the cave faded and we knew it was dark outside. Hrekka slipped out to explore and was gone a long while. As the time passed, we grew anxious, and I'd almost decided to go looking for him when he swam back in, breathless.

He had swum out to find it was indeed dark, but the stars were out. He could see the black silhouettes of the whaling fleet against them. Otherwise the iron monsters showed no lights and were waiting silently, sending an occasional *ping* echoing through the water. One catcher must have located Hrekka, because it started toward him, phosphorous wings of water showing at its bow. He steered himself between a rock and the Wall, and the catcher fell back. He then called out in a hoarse whisper for Ala, Ali, and Ross.

After a while a shadow crossed the stars and Ala descended. The albatross was glad all had made it to the cave, for he'd seen us attacked by the thunderwing before we disappeared underwater. He, Ali, and Ross had separated and searched for us the whole length of the cliffs, afraid we had drowned. On the far side of the Rock Wall the other half of the fleet was still hunting Seis, Fins, and the small Minke whales.

On this side they'd counted several dozen ships waiting silently in the dark for us to come out of hiding. While they talked, the sky suddenly lit up and a bright fire floated in the air over one of the iron monsters. Hrekka and Ala saw a figure point at them from the bow as the catcher started up. With a squawk,

Ala flapped into the air and beyond the mountain peak. Hrekka dove and swam back to the cave.

We were worried by what he said. Men were able to put a light into the sky, making it almost as bright as day. I had seen one of these hanging fires when an oil ship was breaking up in a storm, but I'd never seen one used by whalers. The Council gathered and Hrūna spoke: "There is nothing we can do to stop the hanging fires and dawn is coming. I will go first, and if the hanging fires follow me, so much the better, because it will be dark for the rest of you. I will lead them on a chase they won't forget!"

The pod felt unhappy at the thought of Hrūna exposed to the lights, but we had no choice. To wait for daylight would be far more dangerous.

For a moment Hrūna blocked the dim light of the entrance and then was gone. I followed him out to see what happened. For a minute he raced along the Rock Wall in the dark. Then an artificial star burst and hung high in the air. The *thrug thrug* of engines started and two catchers chased after him. The star floated down into the sea and it was dark once more.

I called softly to the next in line, a young whale named Hranak. He slid away into the dark and I waited. No star appeared, though far away I saw a pinpoint of light where the whalers pursued Hrūna.

Then a mother and her calf swam out. Over the next hour I sent the pod along in twos and threes at wide intervals. It remained dark, and mysteriously no other catchers came during the exit of the rest of the whales. Only three of us remained when Hrekka left and the night abruptly blazed with light. Three hanging fires shot up and three catchers started up after him.

Only Aleea and I remained. With a quick parting hug, I sent her on ahead.

No hanging fire went up.

A short while later I left, racing along the black shadow of that coast, the stars tiny pinpricks above me. I was beginning to think the iron monsters hadn't noticed me, when I heard a faint *ping* and a moment later a hanging fire burst above me. A single catcher roared into life under it.

It was some time before the ship caught up with me, running as close to the mountains as it dared. Its green eye winked and wavered evilly through the water. Now and then it lofted another artificial star. I waited for these to die in the water before rising for a gulp of air. When I did, the whaler always veered close to the cliffs and shot another fire into the air. But I had my breath and was down before it burst.

I called ahead to Aleea, and she answered that no whaler had found her yet. Ahead of her, from the sound of it, there was plenty of pursuit. The ocean vibrated with the noise of the whaling fleet. I sped up and tried not to think of what might happen before the pod reached the ice shelf in the morning. Once or twice I heard explosions far ahead, and each made me wince.

Once I looked up and saw three white shapes flying directly over me, luminous in the radiance from one of the hanging stars. The sight of the albatrosses gave me hope.

At long last, after the alternating dark and light of the manmade stars, the sky grew faintly lighter. Dawn was on its way. The ship pursuing me now sped on ahead. I worried it was after Aleea, but she called back that it passed her as well. Something was happening ahead of us. I heard a confusion of *thrug thrugs*, as of many iron monsters coming together, and three sharp explosions. My throat tightened.

As the early gray grew lighter, I could see the black wall of the mountains and in the distance the dark shapes of ships on the gray water. While the sky flushed pink behind the Rock Wall, the silhouettes of the ships multiplied, and beyond them a pink strip on the horizon marked the ice shelf.

My heart rose at the sight, but not for long. Aleea cried out that the pod was trapped. I spyhopped to see what had stopped the pod short of the ice. From the Rock Wall far out into the ocean a line of catchers lay, nose to tail, blocking the way. From their sides down into the water stretched ropes and nets.

My heart in my throat, I sped forward and caught up with Aleea in the brightening water. She was swimming slowly, and not far ahead swam two or three other familiar shapes. I slipped alongside and rolled against her, encouraging her: "We are close to the ice—and safety."

I hurried on and was gaining on the others when a loud explosion shook the water and a number of cries rose up. Between the line of ships and me, a mountain of water foamed at the surface, with a catcher on either side of it. High spumes of foam flew into the air where something rose and heaved. Then I heard a whale scream. It was Old Hrobo.

Still weak from yesterday, he had been caught in the open and harpooned twice, and the snakelike ropes between him and the bows of the catchers were stretched tight. As I raced closer, I saw the foam turn pink where Hrobo thrashed, and then his spout, tinged with blood, rise into the air, a rose-colored mist that dispersed on the wind. Nevertheless, I heard his faint, quavering voice come through the water as he sang:

> Though the steel harpoon cut home to my heart,
> I shall swim in that Ocean of Light forever
> Where shows no sorrow nor shadow of turning.

He heaved once more and lay still. From out at sea one of the ghastly mother ships started toward the catchers and dropped her jaw to swallow our old singer and friend.

I was too late. The pod called to me not to go closer. Filled with anger, I trumpeted loudly and breached as high as I could. Two other catchers turned toward me, so I dove and shook them off, circling toward the pod. Hrūna and many of the pod had paused in a little cove in the cliffs protected by rocky outcroppings. Mothers and calves lay to the inside. Everyone was in shock at Hrobo's death, and several keened loudly.

Just as I reached them, the Red Bull of the Sun rose in a cleft in the mountain wall and shone on the whaling fleet, which glowed a dull blood color in its light. The calves cried out at the sight. Though silent, the long line of ships stretching out from the wall looked deadly indeed. Nets hung over their sides, reaching to the bottom and overlapping from the stern of one to the bow of the next. Several of the council were deep in talk.

"We cannot circle around the line of whalers and their nets," Hrūna was saying. "We must find some way of going under them."

"I have an idea," I said, and proceeded to explain it. I didn't stop long but called to the pod to watch closely and to follow me as soon as any gap opened in the line of ships. Rising for a deep breath, I swam close to the Rock Wall, approaching the line underwater. Behind me the waters churned as other catchers pursued me. The sea rang with a multitude of *pings*.

I came to the line of ships where the nets, stretched tight, blocked my way. I turned, swimming along the nets, looking for any gaps between them. There were none; they were cleverly overlapped. I bellied along the bottom looking for any spaces under the nets. But they were pinned to the bottom by weights. I glanced up at the line of ship bottoms stretching out toward the horizon and at those of the two catchers following me, their *pings* raining down on me.

I knew I had to act fast.

I swam directly under a ship in the middle of the line. I rose up until I could feel its bottom all along my spine. Then I thrust with my flukes and flippers, pushing up as hard as I could. The catcher rose several feet in the water and rocked to and fro on my back. I heard shouts and cries from inside and the scamper of human feet ringing on the hull. There were splashes to one side, and I saw two men struggling to stay afloat while round white objects were thrown down to them.

Quickly I dove again and came up under the next catcher. Meanwhile the first one had started its engine, *thrug thrug*. When I rose under the second, no one fell overboard, but there were more shouts than ever. Its propellers started at once and I ducked away, fearing for my flukes.

Rising for air, I sang my battle song to encourage the pod:

> *Now I rise to battle, my breath's banner*
> *Bright to behold in the height of the morning.*
> *Hralekana-kolua, on the crest of the comber*
> *Lifts up his cry to creation's four corners.*

The third catcher I struck hard with my head, which hurt for a while. The pain was worth it, since I put a dent in the hull. I rocked the whaler back and forth and its engines started furiously. Dodging the screws I swam to the bottom and looked up. All three catchers had swung out of line and were hauling in their nets.

I cried out to the pod to hurry and to continue hugging the Rock Wall. When at last they reached the nets, they swung toward me and a few at a time—cows and calves first—made it through the gap. Seeing the whales slip through, the remaining ships in the line began pulling up their nets.

Soon the whole pod was past the line of ships and hurrying toward the distant field of ice, now a brilliant white line on the horizon.

The catchers joined in pursuit of us and there were no more protective coves in the Rock Wall. The pod stuck close to the Wall and came up for air only when desperate. Meanwhile, we heard in the distance the swift chopping noise of two thunder-wings and knew they would drop more explosions.

Our only chance was to distract the whalers. I aimed with all my strength at the black bottom of the lead catcher, its wake forming a wide vee behind it. With a loud *thunk* and a sharp pain to my head, I struck it and narrowly missed being slashed by its turning screws. It wobbled and turned hard to starboard.

I dove again and came up under the second one, which tilted and angled off to port. Mustering my remaining courage, I swam within harpoon range and leaped high out of the water in front of it. BOOM, the harpoon roared and flashed past me, the black serpent behind it hissing in the air. It creased my right flipper and cut into the waves beneath me. As I landed on my back, I glanced at the ship's nose, still rocking from my blow. A man with only one flipper raised it over his head, shaking it at me. He was the harpooner.

BOOM, a second harpoon went off behind me just as I dove. The other catcher had fired, but the harpoon fell short. Behind these two catchers came others, attracted by my leap and the sound of the shots. I leaped again, waggling my flippers and turning a complete somersault in the air, the foam flashing silver in the fully risen sun. I was still out of range of the other catchers, while the first two were busy pulling in their harpoons, which glittered wickedly as they were hauled above the surface.

I spyhopped to look for the pod. Several bumps rose by the Rock Wall where mothers and calves surfaced for air. Close by, a catcher fired at a bump that vanished and the harpoon exploded harmlessly against the cliff. Most of the pod, I knew, were between me and the ice, which promised a safe, white haven if we could ever reach it. Three catchers tracked them with echo finders.

The main body of catchers was after me, however. I counted nine. Even two factory ships were closing in on me from farther out. The thunderwing clattered over and dropped more red sticks. I swerved away from where they hit. A sharp pain passed through my head as the sea bottom lit up and the water squeezed me.

I swam a zigzag course—now away from the ice, now toward it, rising when I could to check on the others. Most of the pod were now more than halfway to the ice, so I turned toward it in earnest, still leading the pack of catchers. The one-flippered harpooner was in the lead, crouching behind his gleaming point of death. The black bow of the catcher surged toward me. Gulping a last breath, I dove, aiming at the ice away from where the pod would enter.

It was now full daylight. I could see and hear the jagged ice mountains that had broken from the shelf and begun a strange symphony of howls, groans, and guttural avalanches as they jostled toward open water. Their tops flashed emerald, blue, and white where they glistened in the sun, as rainbows arced and faded in the mist. Never had I seen a more inviting vision of safety and home.

Growing short of air, I swam on. In the distance three explosions sounded, one after the other, and whales cried out in terror. My heart went cold with fear for the rest of the pod. Grimly I struggled on toward them and the ice, trying to escape the fiend following me.

Ahead, the blue, cloudlike hulks of the icebergs turned and ground against one another. There were several miles to go before I would be safe between their walls. The harsh music now sounded sweeter, if possible, than the siren song of the sea people or Aleea's own singing beneath the moon. The music grew louder and pulled me toward those great vague shapes.

Once more I glanced up where the catcher's black nose cut behind me like a shark's. Through the surface I saw the bright tip of the harpoon gleam in the sunlight. I slowed, down to my last reserves of strength. My flippers barely moved. I wanted to give up all effort, but my flukes continued to work, up and down, up and down. Before long, I felt a shadow and looked up as a mountain of ice loomed over me. I aimed to one side where a narrow channel cut between it and its neighbor.

A cry pierced the water. It was Aleea's and it snapped me from my stupor. Fear moved through me as I struck out in the direction of her cry. One long spur of the ice thrust out underwater, blocking the channel. The catcher was right on top of me.

The harpooner apparently knew no fear of the ice, pursuing me this close to it. The icy cliff towered over me and the ship's black shadow slid behind. I wondered if the harpooner had lost his mind—angry as a shark that chews its own flukes.

I turned sharply to skirt the emerald spur and was just entering the channel when I heard a loud crunch and the high-pitched screaming of metal. The black silhouette shivered to a stop and something splashed in the water in front of it. The catcher had

119

struck the spur and torn out its belly. Meanwhile, looking from this depth as tiny as a krill, the harpooner with one flipper wriggled in the water.

Exhausted and starved for air, I floated to the top at a distance from the ship. The catcher was listing badly to port. The crew scrambled into small boats, shouting and pointing at me. Three whale-lengths from the bow, which now sloped down in the water as if aiming the harpoon at the Deep, the one-flippered harpooner floundered badly. He was crying out, but the others didn't hear him. With only one flipper, he would not float for long.

I felt no great love for this man who had tried to kill me, but nevertheless I dove and came up under him. Nearly drowned, he lay stunned and limp on my back. The other catchers stopped at the mouth of the inlet where they waited for the small boats filled with crew, so I dared not take him out that way. There was a small ice floe, however, not far from the catcher, where the crew still clambered into boats. I swam to it, and unsteadily, the cold and shaking harpooner crawled on his flipper and flukes onto the ice. It tilted, until I thought he would slide back into the water, but he heaved himself up and lay in the middle while it rocked back and forth.

His shipmates had seen all this and shouted to him. A boat moved quickly toward the other side of the floe.

Chapter Eleven

Breathing on the surface restored me. Remembering Aleea's cry, I swam between the blue hulks of icebergs toward where I heard it last.

Rounding a spur of ice, I saw her swimming toward me and trumpeted in relief and joy. We rolled as, breathlessly, she told me how she'd watched the harpooner with one flipper chase me. She'd cried out, fearing I wouldn't make it to the ice. Looking back toward open water, we watched the whaling fleet mill about, picking up the men from the small boats. Then side by side we swam between the protective walls to where the rest of the pod was gathered. At last we came to a wide green lagoon far from the edge of the pack and surrounded by tall ice mountains.

In a wild rush, the others greeted us. The last few stragglers were still coming in, and as each arrived, the pod swam up and surrounded the latecomer. Great was the rejoicing and the trumpeting that bounced back and forth between those walls of ice, making strange music with the singing of the ice. Only when one mentioned Old Hrobo did the pod grow silent. That evening, while the moon rose higher and whitened, the keening for Hrobo began and lasted late into the night.

Sadly, one voice rose over the ice:

> Gone is he from the great sea, gone from the restless waves,
> Hrobo the high-hearted, singer of many songs.
> Never will he return where narwhal spears the blue,
> Where dolphin and seal dart, and herring dance in shoals.

It was answered by the others:

> Wide is the sea we cross—or narrow, as One decrees.
> Come, my brother, close, and comfort you by our side.
> Sore is the single heart with none to share its hurt.

Then all together:

> Take him, Bender of Tides, who take the Ocean in tow,
> From whose mouth flow waters out of the fathomless Deep,
> Over that Ocean of Light, where no one living may go.

Only after the keening was over did our voices rise in the Song of Deliverance:

> Wily by the Rock Wall the whalers lay waiting,
> While the dense fog lay dark over the Deep,
> Surprising the pod when they suddenly sailed,
> Crowding cow and calf to cower in the cave,
> Harrying us with harpoon toward the murderous nets,
> Till Hralekana the Bold battered the ship bottoms,
> Broke up the nets—and we burst between them,
> To the ice fled fast while he decoyed the destroyers,
> And all made it safely, all except one.

We sang until the Leaping Whale's flukes lobtailed over the edge of the world.

The next morning, fearing nothing, we slept late. The sun was bright when Ala returned to tell us the whaling fleet was still there in full force. It was only then that we faced our true situation. Though the ice protected us, we had no desire to travel

124

under it. With colder weather coming, we could not break open the breathing holes. Even if we could, the whalers would still follow us with their echo finders, which had not stopped probing for us under the ice. They'd be waiting for us when we had to leave the ice for the open sea.

We started through the ice pack, swimming between the blue and green mountains of ice, taking our time. Outside the ice, the whalers tracked us by echo and sailed along parallel to us.

In a few days, we knew, the icebergs would thin out and we'd be forced to swim under the ice shelf, coming up to breathe at the edge. Our only hope was that the whalers would tire of the chase and go home before winter forced us into the open sea.

Day after day we traveled. It looked as if the whalers would never give up. We guessed by this that the hunt had gone badly for them this year. On the third day they were joined by more ships, the same ones—Ala, Ali, and Ross told us—that had pursued Seis and Fins on the other side of the Rock Wall.

We were only days from where we must head out into the open sea. The adults were silent, wondering what would become of us, when we heard a familiar high *thrug thrug* among the deeper sounds of the whaling vessels. Eagerly Aleea and I swam to the edge of the ice. At first we saw nothing and our hopes fell. Then out from behind one of the factory ships, close to the horizon, appeared a yellow speck. The speck grew to a gleaming yellow shape with a rainbow on the bow. It was the *Rainbow Whale*.

The little ship zigzagged among the slower whaling vessels and drew near us, stopping between the ice and the closest whaler. A row of faces lined the rail. A moment later Mark's yellow hair appeared among them and I trumpeted a greeting, spouting high. He raised one flipper over his head, and Aleea and I swam out from the ice toward the ship. When we did, three catchers cruising near the ice turned toward us.

Someone aboard the *Rainbow Whale* cried out, pointing at them. With his flipper curled around his mouth, Mark shouted to us, drowned out by the surge of engines, and the other crew members ran about the deck. They lowered three yellow rafts into the water. These rafts moved fast, one end rising out of the water. They made a high whining sound where they churned the water at the low end. Mark was in the first, and he and the other crew member had bright orange floats on their bellies and backs.

The three rafts headed straight toward the three catchers, where they bore down on us, their prows cutting the water into white wings. For a moment it looked as if the rafts would collide with the catchers, but at the last instant the catchers turned to avoid them. The rafts circled about, tilting on their white wakes, and again aimed at the bows of the catchers. I was afraid for Mark.

All three ships came to a standstill while men clustered on their noses, shaking their flippers and making a good deal of noise. Below them, the rafts stopped, and holding up a large green cone to his mouth, Mark spoke in a voice loud as a bull whale's.

The catchers backed up and tried to steer around the rafts to where we floated halfway between the ice and the *Rainbow Whale*. My throat tightened as I watched Mark speed up again.

Four times the catchers charged toward us, intercepted each time by the rafts weaving their white wakes over the waves. Finally, the catchers gave up and joined the rest of the fleet. When the last one turned back, Mark followed it out a distance, then circled and sped toward us, the bow of his raft rising high in the air, foam flying where it bounced on the waves. Mark's hair blew back like that of the sea people Torvald described. His face was red from the stinging spray, bright above the orange float around his upper half.

Mark turned off the whining sound and the raft floated quietly up between Aleea and me, bumping against my side. To my surprise it felt soft. Mark climbed onto my back and stretched out by my blowhole.

"Hralekana, old friend, how are you?" he breathed warmly down my blowhole.

"Be well!" I breathed back full into his face, understanding the words of his greeting.

He laughed and rubbed one of my scars. Then I felt drops fall from his face, and he didn't say anything for a few minutes. My throat swelled and I was silent.

When he began speaking again pictures flooded my head, as in the past. Mark and I understood only a few words of each other's speech, but when either sang or spoke, the thoughts made clear pictures in the other's mind. We understood each other very well this way—and so did Aleea and Mark.

Mark had last seen me when I was wounded by the limpet mine. He had a hundred questions. It was Aleea who answered him first.

"We thought we had lost Hralekana," she began softly, and while we lay there, bumping up against the raft, she showed Mark all that had happened since he and I parted on the day of my wounding. He nodded, as the pictures passed through his mind. When she finished, Mark slid into the water and swam down to my wound. I obliged him by rolling on my side.

He swam back to my head and looked me in the eye. "It is al-most healed," he said in a small voice. Other pictures flashed through my mind. There was a light in his eyes.

By this time the other rafts were aboard the *Rainbow Whale* and human voices called to Mark and his companion. The sun had disappeared behind the icebergs to the west, and the pale polar glow would not last long. The water was beginning to mist, and the thousand eyes of the whalers flashed on. A red and a green light appeared on the *Rainbow Whale*.

Mark asked me about the pod, and I briefly told him of our journey under the ice and our ambush by the whalers. He pro-mised to meet me by the ice the next morning and pulled himself over the side of the raft with both flippers. Aleea and I swam back to the lagoon, joined by some who had watched our reunion from the edge of the ice.

At dawn, I swam out from the ice alongside the *Rainbow Whale*. I thumped her affectionately with my tail and immedi-ately heard flippers scrabbling around inside. I dove and swam under her, examining her smooth hide where I'd scraped off the round metal mine months ago. There wasn't even a mark to show where it had clung like a barnacle to her. I rose again, nuz-zling the little yellow ship.

Mark's face appeared over the rail and he whooped with de-light. In a moment he was on my back again. The sun had risen, and its rays were warm in the shelter of the ship. While we spoke, others lowered the three rafts and began to patrol between the *Rainbow Whale* and the whaling fleet. The catchers started up and headed again toward the *Rainbow Whale*. So I swam with Mark back to the ice, one of the rafts close behind.

In the raft was another human whose fur was long and red and glittered in the sun. Mark introduced me to his friend Meg, a female of his species. Except for her long fur, she looked the same as Mark. They wore the same black skin over their own skin, and both had on detachable blue flukes. When she spoke, her voice was higher-pitched and more melodious than Mark's. She climbed on my back and sang "Be well!" down my blowhole and laughed a high silvery laugh.

"Be well, Meg," I replied. "Your fur catches the sun as brightly as a seal's." Apparently she understood what I said, for both she and Mark laughed and she patted my blowhole.

There in the green shadow of the ice wall we three lay the whole morning, catching up on the past months and watching the maneuvers of the catchers and rafts. When Mark said something, Meg added words to it, often humorous, and I could understand her. We all three laughed many times. After an hour of probing to see if they could slip past the *Rainbow Whale*, the catchers gave up, but the fleet still didn't leave.

With pride in his voice, Mark told me that the mission of the *Rainbow Whale* to the islands had been successful. They'd found the island where the gray ships had clustered and men erected a tall tree to hold the metal egg that would explode in a fire as large as the sun. The men had already unloaded the metal egg from the ships and placed it on top of the man-made tree. All that remained for the men to do was to sail the ships to a safe distance. Then the fire would appear in a flash and devour the island and the creatures in the sea for miles around. Its cloud would climb black and red miles into the air and poison the ocean.

But Mark, Meg, and others from the crew of the *Rainbow Whale* sailed in by night and landed on the island. Through a black box like the one aboard ship, they told humans around the world what the men were about to do.

The men from the gray ships tried to talk them into leaving and even carried one or two onto the warships, but other humans responded to what Mark and the crew said over the black box. Before two days had passed, other ships, from different pods of humans, sailed to the island and refused to leave until the large metal egg was removed. Mark said humans all over the world were angry with the men on the warships.

Several days after the new ships arrived, men from the warships carried the metal egg down from the man-made tree and put it back in a ship's belly. The new ships stayed there to make sure they took it away while Mark and the *Rainbow Whale* hurried off to find us. They worried when they found no trace of us by our old feeding grounds and at first feared we'd fallen victim to the pirate whalers to the west.

Although they were almost rammed three times by the pirate whalers, they managed to stop them from hunting with the treacherous nets. The *Rainbow Whale*'s crew cut the nets and hauled in what they could of them, freeing the trapped Minke whales and other creatures. They kept the nets, so these wouldn't float around, a danger to other fish and beasts.

After two days of their interference, the pirate whalers left the region. Having seen no trace of us among the pirates, the *Rainbow Whale* left to sail around the Pole. Mark rightly assumed we'd followed his advice and sought out the feeding grounds on the far side of the Pole. He knew it was late in the season and hoped to meet us on our way back. He guessed the journey would be dangerous for us, for the whaling fleet had a lean season and was determined to make up its losses. When the *Rainbow Whale* found the whole fleet gathered outside the ice field, Mark feared they were too late.

Now that they were here, they would stay by us until the fleet gave up and left or other humans arrived to help us. There were other ships like the *Rainbow Whale* on the seas, from other lands and other pods of humans.

By afternoon Mark and Meg had finished telling us all this. The whaling fleet made no further effort to get past the *Rainbow Whale*, but it was still in position. Mark decided he would steer the small raft between the icebergs to our haven. I pointed out that it was dangerous, since the icebergs shifted unpredictably and ground against each other, crushing anything between them; he could hear their wild music where we lay.

He laughed and said it would be a close squeeze at times, but that they could make it. Aleea and I went before and behind, threading a course for the raft among giant bergs. Only once did the blue and green walls of an ice canyon begin to close on each other. Mark sped up and the raft just made it into a broader passage. As he and Meg left the closing channel, the overhangs on two icebergs met and exploded in a shower of crystals that filled the raft. For a moment Mark was lost in a cloud of mist and ice, but he shook himself free, laughing. He and Meg scooped the ice out of the raft with their rubber flukes.

In a very short time we were at the green lagoon, and one by one I introduced the pod to them. Mark and Meg spoke to the pod, saying special words to each, including all of the calves. Then with much fuss and clamor, Ala, Ali, and Ross flew down and I introduced them. After a lot of coaxing, Ross allowed Meg to stroke his feathers.

"What a beautiful bird!" she exclaimed, and Ross, pleased but embarrassed, shut his eyes and crossed his feet, tripping and falling into the water. The pod laughed aloud and the ice rang with their snorts, clicks, grunts, whinnies, and trills. From that moment, the pod and the albatrosses took Meg to their heart.

It was late in the day and a star or two were out when I said they'd better be getting back to the *Rainbow Whale*. But both Meg and Mark protested they planned to spend the night with us and showed me some extra skins they could put over themselves to guard against the cold.

The moon was nearly full that night, and in its light the ice walls shone as bright as day. We stayed up late with Mark and Meg, the grown-ups talking with them and the calves showing off various tricks. They'd been warned not to splash our human guests.

When the moon was high overhead, the pod joined together in singing. We sang the Song of the Ice, the Song of Cold Waters, and the Song of the Sun and Moon for Mark and Meg. Earlier, when Mark told me of their brave deeds in facing down the ships and the men with the metal egg, I had begun composing a song about their exploits. I whispered it to the others that evening, and when the moon was straight overhead, we surprised our guests with the Song of the *Rainbow Whale*:

> *Following the fierce ships that carried the fire,*
> *It jauntily dared the sharp jaws of danger,*
> *The egg that would eat the ocean all around it.*
> *Fearless, the few faced the mighty many,*
> *Sailed to the island and swiftly took a stand,*
> *Telling the world wrongdoing was under way,*
> *Until proud ships arrived and persuaded the others*
> *To fold up the fire and sail away.*

When we finished, the last notes rang off the ice walls and the moon slid behind a white peak. The stars swam large and bright. Mark and Meg were silent where they lay stretched out on my back, and I felt drops falling from Meg's face.

Chapter Twelve

The next morning Mark and his friend Meg again wove through the thin green channels between the ice mountains, Aleea and I guiding them. When we reached open water, we found the whaling fleet still in position, as was the *Rainbow Whale,* her yellow sides and gaily painted rainbow glistening in the early sun. The crew clapped their flippers when they saw Mark and Meg emerge safely from the ice.

The couple returned briefly to the *Rainbow Whale* before rejoining us by the ice. The catchers made one attempt to come at us, then fell back to wait. Meanwhile, Mark told me the *Rainbow Whale* had spoken with ships all over the globe through her black box and some were coming to help.

The pod was restless to move on and our lagoon was beginning to freeze over at night, so Mark advised that we travel among the icebergs until these gave out and then under the edge of the ice shelf. The *Rainbow Whale* would stay between us and the fleet. We were concerned, of course, about a quick freeze trapping us miles from open water. To guard against that, both we and the *Rainbow Whale* would keep watch at night.

That day we traveled slowly under the icebergs, the *Rainbow Whale* keeping pace with us. The whalers tracked us by echo finder and shadowed the *Rainbow Whale*. So it went for several days while the yellow ship kept our hope up by reporting the progress of the ships sailing to join us.

The water was colder at night and froze, first in a fine film, then in thin sheets, and finally in a solid layer. There were fewer open havens among the icebergs, and the pod crowded together in what breathing spaces we found, or cautiously surfaced outside the ice to breathe quickly and plunge back under.

Then on the third night after we started, the fleet vanished. The next morning we all swam outside the ice, celebrating the freedom of the open sea. But Mark and the crew remained cautious. They had no explanation for the whalers leaving so suddenly and feared it was only a ruse, that they would return. Ala, Ali, and Ross flapped off and vanished over the horizon. They were gone the better part of the morning, returning breathless to say that the fleet was far at sea and steaming full speed away from the ice. At that news, the pod sang and everyone leaped for the first time in weeks, smacking the barnacles off. Watching us, the crew of the *Rainbow Whale* cheered, and together we coasted outside the expanding ice shelf.

The whalers did not return, but the *Rainbow Whale* sailed with us the seven days it took to reach the ice opposite our old feeding grounds. From there, they escorted us for two days out into warmer waters. Often Mark lay on my back as I swam through the rolling waves and we spoke of many things. He was curious about every aspect of the pod's life and I about his life on land. Many new pictures flowed into my head, strange and hard to understand. Often when Mark rode on my back, Meg rode on Aleea's. The two became fast friends, sharing thoughts for up to half the morning. The rest of the pod were growing bolder and invited crew members to ride on their backs.

At the end of the second day, the sky purple in the west, the *Rainbow Whale* stopped and we sang good-bye to Mark and Meg and the crew. Mark and Meg, their flippers entwined, stood at the tail of the ship as she pulled away. Silently we watched her red and green lights vanish into the blue dusk as she headed east to protect the Fin whales from any further assault by the whalers.

A day or two later we said good-bye once again to Ala, Ali, and Ross. Ross tweaked my hump with his beak and launched into the air. The three circled once, cried out together, and beat their slow, majestic way over the horizon.

As the waters grew warmer, our mood grew lighter. The year-ling calves leaped over each other while we traveled, braiding a white wake behind them. At night the flukes of the Leaping Whale fell low to the horizon and disappeared. The sight of an occasional land bird revealed we were nearing the islands, and at night I'd wake as a breeze stole by laden with the smells of tropical fruits and flowers. The day came when someone spied a coconut and the next a water-soaked palm log floated by just under the surface. Some of the pod shed tears at these signs of home, for we had spent a much longer season at the Pole than ever before. The warmth of the water and air felt strange, almost exotic, after so long an absence.

Aleea had swollen to half again her normal size and seemed to swim in a world of her own as she contemplated giving birth. I worried that the calf would prove too large for her. One day she called me to her.

"Listen!" she said, and I pressed close to her belly. Not only did I feel the calf move this time, but I heard a pulse, softer and more rapid than Aleea's, and then a second one. Suddenly, I grew excited. In fact, I dove and threw myself in the air in a wild flip, trumpeting loudly. Surprised, the pod stopped and stared at us.

"Two!" I cried out. "Aleea is carrying twins." Lewtë and Hree-lëa swam over to her, confirming the news. The pod closed about us in a protective circle while I swam close to her side, wishing the long journey were over. Neither of us slept that night, listening to the faint watery noises within.

A day later a familiar peak rose little by little over the horizon, and we all hurried toward the islands of our birth. The sun was bright overhead, and in the distance we heard breakers crashing on the reef that we loved so well. As calves we had fallen asleep to the rhythm of those waves washing over the coral or sliding up the sands and falling back. It was the ocean's lullaby.

Our first night back the stars shone without a moon. Warm and bright, they floated across the heavens like so many jellyfish trailing their rays, showing different colors if one looked at them steadily. In the middle of the night someone cried out and we woke to a shower of falling stars, followed by another. One star streaked right over us and we heard it strike the ocean scores of miles away.

When the moon rose narrow and white a few nights later, the birthing began. A female attended each of the birthing cows. After hours of labor, the calf would emerge quickly, tail first, while the helper caught it on her back, lifting it to the surface for its first breath.

With each birth I grew more excited, while Aleea grew more calm, more distant and faraway. Toward the end of each labor the pod joined together in the Song of Birthing, to encourage the mother and also to welcome the newborn into a world filled with singing:

> Welcome, new one, to the world of water,
> To the air above it and the shining light.

We others, just like you, gather to love you.
Open eye, open ear, to day and night!

May Red Bull, White Cow, leap high over you,
A million stars guide you, twinkling bright.
Now open your mouth and swim to your mother,
Borne up by our song through the water and light.

On the third night, the third calf was born just after sunset. The first two had the usual markings—black with white flippers. The third, however, a calf born to Hrekka and his mate Hweena, was speckled, like Aleea's cousin Hrēta. I thought if Aleea had to wait any longer, she would burst, for I had never seen an expectant mother so large.

At midnight, shortly after moonrise, her belly began to contract and she cried out—not in pain, but in surprise. I swam alongside and steadied her with my flipper. She smiled a large, teary smile at me, interrupted by a sharp pain. I called out for help and Lewtë and Aleea's mother, Kaleea, swam up to support her on the other side and underneath.

The next few hours were hard for Aleea, for each time her belly moved she felt pain. I could hardly bear it, lying next to her while she smiled weakly at me between spasms. It seemed as if I could feel the pain too—but not really—and that thought made me feel worse. What if the calves were too large to pass and she died? I felt helpless beside this great mystery of birth. Through the long hours I listened to her rapid heartbeat and shallow breathing and the occasional long moan that came from deep within.

Hrūna swam up alongside and tried to reassure me, but I saw the worry in his eye. The new mothers were singing softly to their newborn under the moon, not far away. The rest of the pod lay silent in a circle around us.

I recalled my own birth under the moon in those same waters and thought of the Whale of Light deep in the ocean under the world. "Please," I asked silently, "help Aleea and our twins."

I was interrupted by a high-pitched scream. Aleea's belly shook and I saw a tiny tail moving below it. The little flukes moved up and down, and Aleea's mother rose under her belly and pushed. In a second, a small black calf slid out. He had a wide white stripe along each side. He started to sink but Aleea's mother caught him on her back and rose quickly, lifting him out of the water. The moonlight gleamed on his new skin as he lay still a moment. Then he lifted his flukes and brought them down with a slap. At the same moment his high-pitched whistle pierced the night and the tiny cloud of his first breath rose above his head.

I felt a rush of love.

The pod sang,

> *Welcome, new one, to the world of water,*
> *To the air above it, and the shining light.*
> *We others, just like you, gather to love you . . .*

A second scream followed the song. I ducked back under where Lewtë had taken the place of Aleea's mother. Aleea was trembling again and her belly convulsed once, twice. A set of tiny white flukes emerged, flapping up and down. Lewtë rose and pressed against Aleea. Her belly heaved once more and suddenly there was a white calf with a wide black stripe down each side, the mirror image of the other calf. She started to drift down but Lewtë caught her and carried her to the surface. There she whistled as her small, white breath rose toward the moon. Then she slapped both flippers and flukes against Lewtë's broad back.

I immediately went over to Aleea, who was no longer trembling but drifting on her side with a blissful look on her face. She couldn't move for weariness, lying there exhausted. I touched her face lightly and whispered in her ear, "They're beautiful."

Aleea's mother brought the first twin to her and her eyes grew bright with love. In a small voice she crooned a lullaby that blended with the hum of the rest of the pod. Lewtë then brought the white female calf to her other side and Aleea's song leaped an octave to ecstatic trills.

We both nuzzled the twins, taking in their individual scents as we felt their smooth skin. They squealed and turned and snuggled up to us. Blindly they butted up against Aleea, following the ancient instinct.

Flooded with joy, I plunged deep and rose toward the moon that bent and wriggled on the surface—breaching high, trumpeting the news far and wide as water flew from me in a million sparks. I crashed on my back and sped in a wide circle around the pod three or four times.

When I returned to Aleea, both twins lay alongside her, feeding ravenously on her milk, swallowing it in great gulps. That which escaped clouded the water and bubbled blue in the moonlight. I thought of the lines about the mother,

> Flooding the sea with her milk while her calves
> Drink and churn, the stars floating above them.

When they were done, the twins fell asleep, cradled between us on our backs. It was wonderful to feel their small bodies and to hear the light whisper of their breath as we lay side by side.

The next morning I woke to feel the two warm spots on my back taking shallow breaths. Aleea was still sleeping too, so I lay there, fearing to wake them by moving. Then one of the breaths gurgled and whistled. A warm spot wriggled and splashed in front of my nose. Aleea opened her eyes and a second splash followed.

White on black, black on white—the twins looked up at us with bright, innocent eyes. They rolled and bubbled in the water, making happy noises. They nuzzled, then chased each other's tail. Aleea rolled on her side and, quick as a flash, they found her milk, making greedy sucking noises as the water churned pale blue about them.

Aleea looked at me, a light in her eyes. "We must give them names," she said.

"He is dark as the night," I said, "and she is bright as the moon. And yet each has the other's color along the sides."

Aleea thought a moment and said, "We'll call them Hvala and Lūvah."

The names seemed right, and just then Hvala and Lūvah stopped feeding and swam up between us. We nuzzled them, murmuring their names. Each was swollen with milk. Already they seemed larger than the night before.

They fell asleep on my back as Aleea swam off with the new mothers to do some bubble netting of herring. She was ravenous and through the next months fed frequently to replenish the milk the twins took in huge amounts. They drank nearly their own weight every day. Often I would hunt for her, bringing her whatever herring or capelin I'd trapped in my mouth.

All that day and the next, Hvala and Lūvah did nothing but feed and sleep, occasionally paddling under our noses and responding with high-pitched squeals when we nuzzled and tickled them. On the third day, however, they stayed awake longer and began to experiment with flippers and flukes, chasing each other in our shadows. They even tried diving for the first time, going under the surface, rising and blowing out their breath.

Once Lūvah made a rainbow. She squealed with excitement and ducked down to do it again, forgetting to close her blowhole. Up she came, choking and sputtering, and we had to lift her up until her breath cleared. Of course, Hvala had to try the same thing, and the two ducked and blew rainbows all afternoon.

Soon the four mothers spent the afternoons together, while the five new calves eyed each other from their safe shadows, within reach of the large, reassuring flippers. The mothers spoke about what each calf was doing—how much milk he or she was taking, and so forth—remarking about each one's growth and trading advice with each other. They spoke for hours about little else.

The calves grew bolder, swimming out from their mothers toward each other, almost touching before fleeing back to the great, comforting maternal islands. Hvala and Lūvah, of course, had learned to chase each other, duck under, and blow rainbows earlier than the single calves, who watched in curiosity. It was not long, however, before the others one by one entered their circle of play, and within a week there was a noisy circus of new calves splashing and breaching and squealing within the guardian wall of mothers. Farther out, we fathers kept watch for sharks or Killer whales.

Soon the five learned to leap over each other, and then they tried to leap over the grown-ups, sometimes landing with a resounding thump on a sleeping whale's back and sliding off with a whistle. Before long they were diving deeper than their own length and swimming underwater, and soon they discovered the fantastic colors and shapes of plants and animals in the nearby reef. Now they spent every day, all day, swimming in the lagoon, playing the same games that Aleea, Hrekka, and I had played as calves. But I was careful to watch the far side of the lagoon in case they were tempted to swim out of it and down the long slope leading to the Ships' Graveyard where, years before, Aleea and I had surprised the Giant Squid. One day when they were older, I would take them there, but there was no hurry. Meanwhile, we let them play, carefree, in the bright waters of the reef.

Chapter Thirteen

Long and happy were those days in the sun with our new family. Aleea and I took turns watching Hvala and Lūvah and going off with our friends in search of food.

One afternoon while Hrekka and I were hunting for herring, we saw a tiny yellow spot on the eastern horizon. It was the *Rainbow Whale*. We glanced at each other and raced toward her.

She shone golden in the setting sun, with her crew standing in the bow, calling to us and waving flippers. Among them I made out Mark and his friend Meg. A moment later the two were in the water and we rose up under them.

Breathless on our backs, they said they'd found no more sign of the whaling fleet, which the black box confirmed was sailing back to port after a lean season. On their way to another mission now, the *Rainbow Whale* and crew had decided to visit us in our calving grounds and Mark hoped to stay with us a while. That was good news indeed!

Hrekka and I sang the news to the pod. Soon most of the adults swam up, spouting and breaching in welcome. We escorted the yellow ship to the gap in the reef that led to the lagoon; it was just wide enough for her to pass. We held our breath as she squeezed by the jagged coral. Once she was inside and at anchor, the crew swam in the warm waters with us. The half-grown yearlings swam with crew members on their backs, leaping and turning, lithe as dolphins. We gave the rest of the day over to play.

That night, as the moon rose, the humans made a fire on the beach; it sparkled and flashed over the low waves of the lagoon.

The crew made music and sang by the fire, beating hollow instruments shaped like large shells, and the pod in the lagoon sang too, the songs blending under a waxing moon.

The next day the *Rainbow Whale* sailed on, leaving behind Mark and one yellow raft. He explained that Meg was needed aboard ship to study krill and plankton, in whose ways she was wise. Mark anchored his raft in the middle of the lagoon, saying he'd spend both days and nights there, living as much as possible with us.

So began a glorious time when Mark lived and swam among us under that tropical sky. The twins were shy of him at first, but Aleea and I brought them up to his raft. He leaned over and scratched each by the blowhole. When we backed away, they skittered after us, but Mark coaxed them to stay, and soon they did, rolling over to let him scratch their bellies. Carefully, so as not to scare them, Mark slid into the water. Though still small, they were larger than he, and soon all three were rolling together, splashing, tickling, and squirting each other.

It wasn't long before the other calves also gathered around Mark, and the high screams, whistles, and splashing grew so boisterous that twice I had to rescue my friend: he was choking on the water and they hadn't noticed.

That first night, the pod gathered around Mark to ask about Meg and to say how much they missed her. They also asked if she were his mate, and he told them she wasn't yet, but he hoped she would be. There was much excitement at this discovery, and after the noise died down, all wished them well and a long life together with many calves.

Some also asked him about human calves and how they were born. Could they swim from the first day and how long did they take milk? We were surprised to hear that human calves cannot move upright for two years, and that they stay with their parents almost twenty years before going off on their own.

The longer Mark was there, the more fond of him the twins grew, and Aleea too. Often he'd spend the afternoon with them, lying on Aleea's back, helping her keep an eye on her charges while the two of them talked for hours.

In Mark's honor, we planned a day of games at the time of the full moon. He brought his raft out of the lagoon into the wide waters which, calm that day, stretched to the horizon without a wave. While the Red Bull of the Sun rose fiery in the east, we performed a Sunward Leaping. Several adults leaped up the track of the rising sun until each silhouette was a small black speck against its broad disk and appeared to vanish into the sun. Next we had the Braiding Leap, in which adults leaped over one another, weaving a tremendous wake that stretched for miles.

We grown-ups gladly became slides down which the calves wriggled and whistled as they flew off our flukes into the water. After the new calves were used to this, Hrūna and I curled our flukes around each and lofted them one by one into the air, where they spread their white flippers and appeared to fly. Hvala and Lūvah loved it. Hrūna and I launched the twins together. Side by side they arced through the morning sun, whistling as they flew. Watching us, Mark asked if we might launch him the same way. He weighed so little I had to be careful not to flip him too far. He spread his flippers, arcing high and executing a neat dive. Breathless, the twins swam up and begged for more, and Hrūna and I sent them off over and over until we could barely lift our flukes.

The pod moved through the customary events of rolling, breaching, and aerial flips, but by late afternoon had settled into storytelling and singing solos.

We rested a few hours in preparation for the gloria. Mark lay exhausted on my back. Just before moonrise the bulls descended into the Black Deep and, as the moon broke the horizon, rose slowly toward the surface singing to the cows, who answered us in chorus. Mark was in his raft in the middle of the females, holding a black box he'd earlier promised would catch our song and preserve it so that we could hear it again. Roots attached to what looked like rocks hung out of the raft down into the water—to pick up the sound, he said.

When we reached the surface, the moon was bright over the waters, which flashed with moonfire. The bulls' voices broke the water, deep and yearning, while the cows' rose in ever higher spirals and trills until male and female met and blended and broke against the stars. Even the calves contributed whistles and short, high notes.

Then the pod broke apart, swimming toward every point of the horizon, voices answering one another in counterpoint as they faded. After a short space of silence we turned around and moved back toward the center, one or two voices rising in solos or duets until the whole pod met in a great roaring chorus. Again silence, and again a song far off. Once more all voices swelled together. And so the night of the gloria passed until the moon sank, a pale shell, in the brightening dawn.

It was then Mark surprised us by letting us hear what he had saved on the black box. The music came back to us under the water, vibrating from the stone-shaped objects hanging by roots down from the raft. For a moment some of us thought the pod had begun singing again or that another pod had come among us, stealing our songs.

We heard ourselves with some pleasure, but then we asked Mark to stop, as we needed the silence that always followed our song—and to sleep, exhausted as we were. Many of the pod questioned the value of this box that copied our song since, as they said, we could always repeat the music ourselves, with new variations. Mark said that having made a copy, he could play our song for humans on land. He hoped that they would understand us better and perhaps no longer hunt us. But to hear ourselves did seem strange and made us feel odd—the music squeezed inside that black box, not rising freely to vanish into the moon and the emptiness between the stars.

The following day Mark asked me to take him to the Ship's Graveyard. I did so, holding one of the raft's snakelike ropes in my mouth and towing it. It was a short swim around the island and over the sloping bottom to where the ships had burned and sunk long ago in that struggle between men. Mark grew quiet as we approached. He held over the side a clear shell through which he could look down at the bottom. We stopped first above the old wooden ship where Aleea and I found the treasure and next over the giant gray ship. Mark was silent at first and then made a whistling sound with his lips.

"How many ships are down there?" he asked.

"I don't know," I replied. "More than there are whales in our pod."

Mark put on his black outer skin and hard, yellow fish bladders on his back. Pinching his blowholes together, he slid over the side backwards and the two of us dove to explore the iron monster where Aleea and I, as calves, had disturbed the Giant Squid.

The long gray ship, flaking with rust, looked as formidable as ever when we settled by it on the bottom. We were in the Blue Deep and shadows lurked everywhere. The hole in the side of the ship was as black as I remembered it. At the memory of the squid a shudder passed from my blowhole to my flukes.

While we gazed at the dark hole, a school of capelin swam into it and, a minute later, swam out, with nothing chasing them. That was a good sign.

Mark had with him a light he held in his flipper or attached to his head. He also carried a long stick with sharp metal points on one end. Turning on the light, he entered the dark hole. I followed, avoiding by inches the jagged edges. It was a tight squeeze. I called out in a loud voice, "Be well!"

"BE WELL! . . . Be well! . . . well . . . well . . . well . . ." the echoes returned from far within. This time, with the light, it was easier to see the stacks of wooden things, though there was barely room for me to move around them. Again, on the floor lay the round bones with three holes I'd seen before. When Mark shone his light on these and some long, thin bones, he shook and let out a cloud of bubbles. His face grew whiter through the glass mask. We also saw large metal coconuts with spines like those of sea urchins. Mark said to stay away from these for they might explode.

We passed around a small mountain of wooden things and found the dark opening to the second belly of the ship, where Aleea and I had met the Giant Squid.

Cautiously, we moved up to the opening, but it was now too small for me to pass. Mark went ahead; a moment later, I heard him scream. Something flickered large and white on the bottom. I watched while he played the light over a huge pile of bones heaped together against one wall of the belly. He turned and hurried out, his face pale in the light from the lamp.

"Let's go up," he said, gasping for air.

At the surface he removed the glass from his face and breathed for a long minute before speaking. "I think I found the place where the Giant Squid made its nest."

"I saw," I replied. Neither of us said anything after that. We dove down once more so that Mark could examine the ship's back, including the long metal logs that stuck out at angles from the reeflike structures. The dead iron monster stared into the blue water through a hundred empty eyes.

From there we traveled over the whole graveyard. Mark looked down through the clear shell, and at almost every ship he decided to go down. Some of the ships lay on their sides, others upside down or in two pieces. Most were right side up, and these he especially wanted to explore. They were different sizes, but most had no iron logs on top. All had holes in them and showed signs of fire; many had metal parts as twisted as the legs of an octopus.

I told Mark of the Seeing I had my first time there—of the fire that belched from the iron logs, the white explosions, and the orange flames that sank the ships; of the giant birds that dropped fire from above; and of the men crying out in pain and jumping in flames into the sea. He was silent for a long time.

We tried entering the belly of a smaller ship, but I found it too narrow. When I thumped my flukes against the side, we heard a scurrying sound, and a small octopus hurried out, pulsing red and blue, its eyes shiny with fear.

On the way back I took Mark to the old wooden ship where Aleea and I had found the yellow pebbles and colored stones years ago. But there was no treasure left in its belly, except for a single pebble I uncovered with my flipper. A larger hole had been cut into the side. Mark looked at it closely and said men had done this.

He was even more quiet on the way back and looked sad. I knew that the Ships' Graveyard and the tale of the battle from my Seeing had given him much to think about.

Chapter Fourteen

We were returning to the far side of the reef when something shot out of the water beside me and landed on my back with a squeal and a thump. A second squeal flew out of the water and thumped into the first, and both tumbled down my flukes into the foam—white over black over white. Behind me, Mark laughed. We'd been ambushed by Hvala and Lūvah.

The twins rolled over on the surface, snorting and splashing. While we watched, three more small shapes leaped over my back and circled Mark on his raft. The calves had found the way out of the far side of the lagoon. They rose up and slapped the water, splashing him and flipping backward.

Mark laughed again and removed from a transparent shell some pink shrimp he tossed into the water. Soon all five returned to his raft, begging for more.

"Hvala, Lūvah, Hreena, Hriki, and Hrolpa," he said each name as he dropped shrimp in their mouths. The five chorused thanks and hurried off to breach in a row for him.

"They're getting older," I said to Mark. "Tomorrow I'll take them to the Ship's Graveyard. It's time they learned more about the ocean around us and about humans."

On the following day Hrūna and I led the calves to the Ship's Graveyard. I was feeling sad, for Mark had heard through the black box in his raft that the *Rainbow Whale* was returning for him that afternoon. He did not go with us to the Ships' Graveyard but stayed behind to gather samples of water and sand in his clear shells as part of his ongoing study of the ocean.

As we returned from the Graveyard, I saw the familiar shape of the *Rainbow Whale* in the lagoon. Mark was lifting his things from the raft to the deck, where Meg took them. I could see from their faces how happy they were to be together again. Nevertheless I felt hollow inside, knowing that these two friends would soon leave. The calves sensed my mood, for they didn't splash or call out to Mark the way they usually did.

When I swam up to the raft, Mark and Meg were smiling. He stretched out full length on the edge of the raft and stared me in the eye.

"Old friend, would you like to come with us to the mainland?" he asked.

In the twitch of a fluke my sadness was gone. For a moment I couldn't utter a sound, my head flooding with pictures of us traveling together. I slapped the water, went under, spouted, and bellowed my answer. Watching us, Hvala and Lūvah grew excited and leaped over me, narrowly missing the raft, which nearly swamped. Mark stood up, drenched, and we both laughed. He described the journey he had in mind, and I then took the twins back to Aleea.

Aleea was silent when I told her what Mark had proposed. She looked away for a while, then turned to me, smiling. "I knew the day would come," she said, "when you would wish to go with Mark and the *Rainbow Whale* back to their home. Go and be glad. Only do not stay too long."

"I won't," I promised. "I'll return before the next full moon."

The following morning when the dawn was just a ghost of gray in the east, the *Rainbow Whale* started her screws. *Thrug thrug*, they churned the waters of the lagoon, and soon we were headed out to open sea, the pod surrounding us.

A few miles out, I nuzzled Aleea and pressed the twins close, one under each flipper. We sang good-bye, and by the time the sun rose, the pod were tiny specks on the horizon. In its rays I saw Hvala and Lūvah breach three times, their flippers flashing pink. I felt a twinge of worry at the sight, for they were still young and needed protection. But I had faith in Hrūna and Hrekka, who had promised to take special care of them.

The ship ran day and night, stopping sometimes for several hours while I rested or fed on herring. I often nuzzled the *Rainbow Whale's* smooth skin or, for a prank, thumped her as we traveled. Mark and the others climbed down to lie on my back and talk as we sailed along.

After a number of days we were in sight of a land mass, blue on the horizon. Sails white as gull wings skimmed the waters along the coast, and Mark warned me to stay underwater, so as not to attract attention. We saw many iron monsters at a distance, and the water was noisy with the sound of metal thrugging, clanging, and groaning. As we moved north along the coast, the eyes from human dwellings flashed gold in the setting sun and shone many colors at night. The dwellings lay in white clusters along the coast or dotted the mountains behind.

One afternoon we approached a gap in the coast where ships were going in and out. The noise they made was astounding. Before reaching it the *Rainbow Whale* pulled into shore, anchoring in a small channel between a cliff and an island. Mark climbed overboard onto my back.

"We'll wait here overnight and go on in the morning. The water inside is not as clear and pleasant as that outside the bay. You'll have to see if you can stand it."

I was dozing off in the late evening sun when—*thud, thud, thud*—I felt something, or things, land on my back. I heard a high squeaky chatter and felt a scrabbling about before whatever they were slid off into the water.

161

"What the . . . ?" I spouted, rising high in the water. There was a splash by my right eye and out of the foam popped a funny whiskered creature, staring, scratching its head, and shaking water out of its ears all at once.

"Excuse—excuse them, please," it uttered, then shot off through the water. I felt the three creatures scrabbling at my flukes now, trying to climb up my back.

"Okey, Otey, and Rok—stop that and come here!" the furry creature called in a high, excited voice.

In a flash he was back, inches from my eye. "Ex—excuse them, they're only pups. Imp—impossible ones!" He rolled his eyes and swam around to where the three were still scrabbling. In a second he was back with three small copies of himself, never still, chasing each other in a circle around him, whistling and squealing in tiny, high-pitched voices. He ignored them, floating on his back and staring at me upside down. He was a sea otter. His fur was dark but his face white with the years. He looked too old to have pups.

"Ok-Okachi is the name," the sea otter said, twisting his head to keep an eye on his charges.

"Okachi?" I asked, in disbelief. That was the name of the sea otter Hrūna had met years ago when he rescued Lewtë from the lagoon where men held her captive. Staring at him, I told him who I was.

"Hrūna's son?" Now it was his turn to be surprised. He swam up and down my length and let out a slow whistle. "Is it possible . . . ?" he asked, his voice failing.

At my invitation he and his grandpups climbed onto my back, where Okachi obligingly removed barnacles while he talked. The three pups slid down my tail and climbed up to slide again. The tips of their tiny flippers felt good as they scratched and scrambled over my thick hide.

162

"It's a sad—it's a sad thing, eh?" Okachi said, picking at an especially tough barnacle. Before he could go on, there was a sharp bark to my port side and two more otters appeared. Okachi introduced them as his daughter Kiki and her mate Atachi, parents of the pups. They scrambled up and soon all three were chattering, removing barnacles, and taking an occasional slide off my flukes with the youngsters.

At last, when he could concentrate, Okachi continued: "It's sad that the water inside the bay is too bitter to live in. Too many iron monsters—especially those carrying oil—and too much that smells and strangles flows into the bay from the city of men, eh? We otters moved out here a number of years ago after Okeela grew sick from the water . . ."

He paused and stared at the horizon. Okachi went on to recount how up and down the coast, the story was the same. Sea otters had to move away from the cities of men. And the mouths of some rivers, once fertile with fish, now spewed forth poisons. Men were cutting down the ancient forests on the mountainsides and what drained from the land there muddied the rivers and made them unlivable for fish and other animals. The salmon no longer swam up those rivers to breed.

His face grew grave and still for a moment. To the far north, he'd heard, an oil ship had broken apart and spilled deadly oil along a rich and fertile shoreline, killing countless fish and birds, and thousands—yes, thousands—of sea otters. His family held absolutely still while he related this. One of the pups whimpered.

Okachi looked at him tenderly and said, "There are mussels under us." In a flash the pups were gone, and their grandfather smiled.

In a minute Okey, Otey, and Rok surfaced, each carrying a mussel in his mouth. Okachi interrupted his story again and dove

163

for a stone. Lying on his back, the stone balanced on his belly, he cracked open the mussels for his grandpups. After gulping these, they tried to imitate their grandfather. It was humorous to watch them attempt to balance stones on their bellies. These inevitably slipped off, and squealing, the three dove after them.

All this time the *Rainbow Whale* had stayed at a distance while Mark and Meg watched us through short black tubes pressed to their eyes. Now she edged closer.

The ship's presence alarmed the otters at first, but they warmed to the crew after I introduced them. Soon they were showing off for them. The crew were busy making images of the otters with little boxes that made a clicking noise and flashed a light. Mark had once made an image of my head with one of these, but it was too small for me to see.

The light faded to a long red strip in the west and a star or two were out before Okachi finished talking. He whistled, and Okey, Otey, Rok and their parents lifted their heads out of the water. After a dozen good-byes, the otters swam toward a cove behind the cliff, six small white streaks on the water.

Chapter Fifteen

Lights shone in the eyes of the *Rainbow Whale*. Mark, Meg, and the crew said good-night and disappeared into the belly of the ship. In the gathering dusk I heard the voices and movements of the crew through the hull, her lights glowing on the water, and for a moment I felt lonely. Above, the sky was clear and swarmed with stars like a bubble net of herring. A thin moon rose, showing only her flukes, as we say.

Then it came to me from somewhere out to sea—the soft rhythm of whales rising, taking breath, and diving. I froze, listening. There were a number of them, a whole pod.

Eagerly I swam out from the island channel. On the horizon, silver in the moonlight, rose and sank a line of spouts, one after another, of a kind I had not seen before. They certainly did not belong to Humpbacks, nor Blues, nor Sperms, Seis, Fins, or Minkes.

"Be well!" I trumpeted and swam to them through the silken night waters gleaming with the reflections of a hundred stars.

"Be well!" came back a chorus of a dozen voices. In a minute I was among them. Although their shape was that of baleen whales, they were smaller than Humpbacks and a mild gray in color.

The pod stopped and stared at me. I introduced myself and several shook their flippers in disbelief.

"Welcome, Hralekana, and please excuse our surprise," said one with a white scar along his side, "but you are larger and different in color from any Humpback we have seen. I am Graygar, leader of this pod. From your look, I would guess you haven't seen the likes of us before, either. We're Gray whales."

He explained that Gray whales lived along this coast and in the spring moved from the warm South toward the Pole. But they rarely went far from the coastal waters, which gave them an abundance of food to eat—though less than they once did.

It was a beautiful night, and lonely for my kind, I joined the friendly Grays. I swam between Graygar and his mate, Galeeta, an even softer, pearl color. Starlight shimmered on their backs while we traveled in an offshore breeze rich with the scents of trees and flowers.

"This coast looks as if it's rich with fish and shrimp," I ventured. "Yet you say there is less than there used to be?"

"Yes, sadly so," Graygar sighed. "Even as our people have increased—no longer hunted by men in these waters—the fishing fleets have depleted our food."

"And what the fishermen leave," Galeeta added, with anger in her voice, "is dying or moving away because of the poison that comes down the rivers into the ocean. Man is an animal who befouls his own waters."

"Yet, I know some humans who are good, who wish to keep the waters clean," I said.

Graygar's and Galeeta's voices rose with a note of hope. "Yes, we do know some humans like that. The winter before last they saved two of our calves, Grahant and Guha, who fed too long in the polar sea and were trapped under the ice far from open water.

"They came in a small yellow ship," Galeeta continued, her voice tight with feeling, "and cut a hole in the ice so our calves could breathe and then more holes leading toward the open sea. They saved Grahant's and Guha's lives."

"Other men came too, after a while," Graygar added. "Many helped them."

We swam in silence for a moment before I said, "I know that ship and the humans on it. In fact, we are only a short swim from it."

Graygar and Galeeta stopped, open-mouthed.

"We are?" they both exclaimed.

So it was that Mark, Meg, and the crew woke in the middle of the night to find thirty whales gathered around the *Rainbow Whale*, blowing their silver breath into the air while stars gleamed and winked off their backs.

Though the Grays did not sing (not what we Humpbacks would call singing, anyway), they managed a short chorus of groans and grunts expressing their thanks. Grahant and Guha, now yearlings of good size, shyly swam up to the boat to be stroked. Both were silent, but they rolled over on their backs and the crew scratched their bellies.

While we lay there, I relayed to Mark the meaning of what the Grays sang to the crew—and to the Grays what the crew said in return.

Graygar gazed thoughtfully at the entrance to the bay, where the air glowed red from the lights of the city of men: "The water in that bay holds many things that can turn the brain," he said, ominously.

"What do you mean?" I asked.

"Several years ago a Humpback swam in there hoping to find a way through the land mass to the other side of the world. His pod tried to discourage him, but he dreamed that the bay was actually a channel dividing the land mass in two. Since none could tell him for sure that the bay was only a bay, with no other outlet, he was determined to find out for himself.

"Once in the bay, he traveled two days without finding an end to it. The farther he swam, the more confident he was of his dream, and his hopes climbed high. Though the water tasted foul and the air above it grew difficult to breathe, he felt it was worth the discomfort to find a new way to the other side of the world.

"When he came to the end of the bay, he refused to believe it was the end. He thought he must have made a wrong turn, so he swam back and forth, trying in every cove and inlet to pierce the continent. The poisons in the water finally made their way to his brain and clouded his judgment, for he could no longer remember which direction he had tried and which he had not. At last, totally confused, with mad phantoms of a sea channel swirling in his brain, he swam up a freshwater river.

"Fortunately, humans who were kind to whales found him and did not kill him, but in small boats and with thunderwings tried to warn him back to the open sea. When this failed, they pushed him downriver. Confused and frightened, he kept trying to swim back up, though he would soon have been stranded in the shallows. Yet he now hallucinated he was a land creature and could crawl out onto the land.

"Again and again, the humans pushed him back to deeper water. At last they succeeded in moving him through the bay and out into the open sea, where after two days his head cleared and he told us the whole story. Though bruised, cut, and disappointed he had not found a way to the other side of the world, he was satisfied he now knew the shape of the bay. His desire to explore and his yearning for the land had nearly killed him. Yet he was pleased to have come closer than any other whale to the interior of the land."

All the while I related to him the Grays' story of the Humpback, Mark looked thoughtful. Finally, with a sigh he told me that he could understand how the Humpback's brain was affected by the water of the bay. He said that not only were the poisons in the water worse than before, but also those in the air, which sometimes were visible in a cloud over the cities of men. In places these poisons descended in a rain and killed the trees of the forest, stripping them of their leaves. His father had spent his life learning about these poisons and trying to get rid of them.

Meg said there were even more frightening events taking place. In some parts of the world men were cutting down the forests and burning them so that dark clouds of smoke ascended high into the heavens. The smoke thinned out, but an invisible part stayed in the air, trapping heat from the sun. This meant the whole earth might warm and the polar ice might melt in the spring and no longer freeze in the winter. The polar ice shelf could disappear. Not only would the krill die, but the ocean would flood the land.

As if that weren't bad enough, Mark added that men put a poison into the air that let dangerous rays of the sun come down to the earth's surface. These rays actually caused animals and humans to sicken and die. Everyone was silent then, while the thin silver flukes of the moon headed downward on her long leap across the sky.

Thanking Mark and Meg and the rest of the crew, Graygar said the Grays had better be on their way. They headed north in a long chain and I joined them for the rest of that night. Mark and Meg stood long by the rail, as they told me later, till our spouts faded into the silver waves. The flukes of the thin moon were near the edge of the world when they went below deck again.

I swam with the Grays until long after the moon fluked and the gray dawn spread from the east. We spoke of many things, and I told them of our under-ice journey the winter before and heard much of their recent history. Talked-out at last, we said good-bye in the early light and I turned back toward the *Rainbow Whale*.

I was enjoying the solitude and thinking over many things from the night's encounter when high-pitched whistles and clicks told me that a school of Bottle-nosed dolphins was headed toward me. I groaned and said good-bye to silence. When they spotted me, they turned as one, leaping out of the sea. Soon the dolphins were circling, leaping over and under me, continuing their chatter among themselves.

A white flash passed in front of me, stopped, and swam up to my left eye. "Well, I'll be a speckled herring!" it exclaimed.

"Whitefin!" I cried, recognizing the white dolphin I met years ago as a calf.

"I was right," Whitefin said, looking up and down my length and whistling. "It turned out not so bad to be different from the rest, eh?"

"I've remembered those words of yours," I said, smiling at the old dolphin.

"Scallop! Marmo!" he called out suddenly, rushing out of sight. In a moment a blue and a marbled blue and white dolphin appeared—my father's other old friends. They too marveled over my size and color, and while the rest of the dolphins danced and leaped about, the three caught me up on news of the ocean.

It was amazing, what they'd heard. They knew about my captivity in the tidal pool and my rescue by Mark. They knew of my visit with Stripes to the dying sea on the other side of the world. They'd heard of my rescue of the *Rainbow Whale* from the exploding limpet mine and how the *Rainbow Whale* had stopped the warships from exploding the giant metal egg on the island.

172

But they hadn't heard yet about my recovery from the wound, which caused them great wonder. They knew our food had been decimated by the oil spill, but they hadn't heard about our journey under the ice nor our rescue by the *Rainbow Whale*. I had the pleasure of telling them of these. I also told them what the Grays had told me, plus what Mark and Meg had said about poisons in the air. They knew about the warming temperatures and the burning forests and had an even more frightening story about a burning.

Six months earlier they'd visited a warm, nearly landlocked sea on the far side of the world, not far from the dying sea I'd explored with Stripes. While they were swimming in these pleasant waters, they saw many gray iron monsters. From these, thunderous birds with fire in their tails continually took off and returned to perch. Metal objects like shooting stars roared and shot off into the night from these ships.

There was so much noise that the dolphins had decided to leave that shallow sea, when something strange and awful happened. They were swimming close to shore when a river of oil began to pour into the water. Quickly it spread over miles of sea and then caught on fire. No ship had wrecked to cause this spill. It looked as if humans on shore were trying burn up the ocean.

Black clouds of smoke rose everywhere. When the dolphins leaped into the air to look inland, they saw hundreds of fires, each belching a column of smoke into the sky. Soon the sky was covered with black clouds and the air was thick with smoke. Birds and animals caught in the greasy tide cried out for help as they suffocated. It looked to the dolphins as if the whole world were on fire. Terrified, they fled as fast as they could out the narrow entrance to this sea. Even outside the straits, where the sky still shone blue, it was hazy, and looking back, they saw massive clouds of smoke roll on the horizon.

Marmo shook his head and waggled his flippers, rolling his eyes. "It seems that man is trying to burn up both the land—his home—and the water, our home. Indeed, we think he has at last gone completely insane."

By this time we were drawing close to land, and I invited Whitefin, Marmo and Scallop and their pod to visit the *Rainbow Whale*. They did, moving up to her hull and greeting the crew with much noise and enthusiasm, permitting the crew to touch them and swim with them. Marmo and Scallop performed tricks from their days of captivity and even allowed Mark and Meg to ride on their backs. After an hour of acrobatics, they circled the ship three times and sped off south and west.

It was midmorning, and Mark decided to enter the bay. I followed, underwater. Several large ships, one a giant warship with thunderwings perched on its top, went in just before us and the channel was still turbulent from its passing. The water grew murkier and obscured the hull of the *Rainbow Whale*. I followed her white wake and the familiar *thrug thrug* of her propeller. The sounds from the other ships nearly drowned that out, and my head ached from all the noise. My eyes burned and I found it hard to keep them open.

After a while I had to rise, and I swam alongside the *Rainbow Whale* so I wouldn't be as noticeable. Before I knew it, we'd passed the entrance and the bay stretched in all directions, surrounded by lowlands, hills, and mountains purple in the haze. No wonder that other Humpback had thought this bay was a passage to the other side of the world.

But what caught my attention was the city of man. There, close by, rising in the early morning sunlight, human dwellings towered into the air like ships standing on end, filled with thousands of eyes gleaming in the brilliant sun. They thrust up like giant spikes of coral, and in as many colors as a coral reef—white, yellow, aqua, gray and pink. Everywhere was noise and the flashing of bright eyes. Mechanical beasts ran along passages between the dwellings, and hundreds of humans crept along on hind flippers. The mechanical beasts swallowed these in some places and disgorged them in others, apparently unharmed.

The *Rainbow Whale* had stopped mid-channel and Mark came up on deck to see if I was all right. I told him the water burned my eyes. Just then, *BOOO-EEEP*, an iron monster blew a warning behind us. We turned to find it bearing down on us. A man on its nose was shouting. The *Rainbow Whale*'s engines roared and she swerved to one side while I dove. The huge wake of the ship moved over me and the shadow of the *Rainbow Whale* bobbed on it.

My eyes stung again, but I followed the little ship underwater as long as I could. Finally, I thumped her yellow hull with my tail as a signal and rose. When I spouted, water seeped into my blowhole and burned it. We were not far from some ships that lay along the shore while giant metal claws reached down through their backs and pulled things from their bellies. The water tasted of dead fish as well as burned oil. Everywhere traces of oil spilled in dull rainbows across the surface. The badly decomposed body of a gull floated a flipper's length from my eye.

Mark bent over the rail, looking worried. His plan had been that I follow the ship far up into the bay, where it always docked.

"I don't think you'd better come," he said. "The water might do you permanent harm. We'll turn around and take you back to the open sea."

I was disappointed I wouldn't see the home of the *Rainbow Whale*, but I had a bad feeling about going farther into the bay.

As we were talking, humans on the docks cried out in loud voices. A few gathered on a dock, looking at me and pointing. A minute later they had grown to a crowd. Three clambered into a small boat by one of the pilings and rowed out toward us.

"Dive and follow us," Mark yelled to me as the *Rainbow Whale* started her engine.

The water burned again as I swam toward the mouth of the bay, but I didn't dare surface for fear of attracting more attention. It was wonderful to see the water clear up and to feel it soothe my eyes. Between the island and the cliff I rose and breathed clean air at last.

I stayed there another day with Mark and the crew, who were taking water samples at various places and times. The water in the bay, they said, had grown worse very recently. There'd been a small oil spill half a year ago. As if to illustrate the point, a huge oil tanker slid past us into the mouth of the bay, dwarfing the other ships around it and sending a high wake to rock us.

While we talked, Okachi and his family swam out to visit again and to slide down my back. The pups grew very friendly and even allowed Mark and Meg to scratch them on their bellies and behind the little bumps on their heads that were their ears.

That night, as the moon rose, showing more of her flukes than the night before, I left the ship, with Mark and Meg standing at the rail. After our time together, it was hard to say good-bye, and the three of us could barely speak. I saw water on their faces glitter in the moonlight. The two pressed their flippers together as I swam off under the stars, singing the Song of Farewell:

> *Wherever on the waters the winds shall find you,*
> *Wherever the moon or the sun shall move. . .*

And I heard them answer:

> *Deep in my heart I will breathe deeply with you*
> *The breath of the one who made you and keeps you.*

Mist drifted across the water as I looked back. It opened once, and I saw Mark and Meg motionless on the side of the little ship, flippers raised in farewell.

Then the mist closed over them and I plunged into the cold, sweet waters.

Chapter Sixteen

While I swam through the cool waters of the night, I thought about the bitter waters and clouded air of the bay. If man had so polluted the land he lived on and the waters within and around it, he would soon no longer be able to live there. It came to me that he might have to escape to the sea to live, as had our ancestors eons ago. The thought of men migrating to the sea to live disturbed my sleep for many nights.

Perplexed by it all, I decided not to return to the islands but to seek first Hralekana's cavern and spend some time thinking over all I had learned. The days were growing longer and brighter, and each night above me the moon waxed larger among her school of stars. I swam swiftly, without rest, and after a number of days plunged once again down into the Black Deep to find the glowing entrance to Hralekana's cave.

As I passed down through the Green Deep and Blue Deep, I thought of my last plunge there, in mortal danger. But now I was vigorous, and descending to it was an easy matter. I loved that cave, and as I passed between the glowing walls, I felt a great peace and contentment flow through me.

To further focus my thoughts, I began uttering my word over and over, letting go of distracting thoughts when they arose, quieting my mind to listen in that dim light. I released all concerns as they rose in my mind: my worry for the safety of the pod, especially Aleea and the twins; my fears about the diminishing krill and the state of the ocean water; and last, my concern for Mark and Meg, as well as those humans who seemed bent on destroying earth, air, and water.

I don't know how long I was there before it came to me, first as a whisper. I grew alert and strained to hear it—a murmur of music on the edge of hearing. It faded, then was there again—just snatches of it, but enough to give rise in me to a great longing:

> *Come to our mountain where land and sea marry,*
> *Where water and rock join and retreat . . .*

There was no mistaking it: the song of the mermen and mermaids. I swam closer to the entrance of the cave:

> *The bitter cold sea and the hot sun above you*
> *Will no longer burn where our bright hair floats over you.*

The music seemed to pull at me, and I swam out of the mouth of the cavern into the Black Deep. There the words came clearly:

> *Marry in the music that murmurs like a river*
> *Where we swim in our bright golden caverns forever.*

I had only heard that singing, faint and far off, twice before—once on the night Aleea and I wove our breaths together in our vow, and once when I was delirious from my wound. Now it sounded clearer than both those times. I knew however far off the sea people were, that they were calling to me, and that I needed to go to them. I knew that whatever it was I had come to discover in the darkness, whatever I was listening for, would come to me through their song.

I swam through the Black Deep, and the song grew louder and faded, just as it had for Aleea. When it faded, I shifted direction to follow, but I often lost it. Then it would come again as a whisper. It led me through many twists and turns:

> Look for us now where the sea currents flow,
> Where the dark waters over you twist and twine
> Around and around till you do not know
> Where you are going. Lost, you suddenly find
> The way you are looking for. . .

Such verses teased and riddled me, and yet guided me:

> Where the winds blow high you will all at once find us,
> Where they blow and yet where the waves grow still,
> In the dark cave where the sunlight glitters,
> In the still Deep where the music is loudest.

A long time passed and still I was in the dark. The song had faded to a murmur. Then far above me I saw a flash of light, a pinpoint, and I rose toward it where it disappeared. After a while it appeared again, larger this time, and did not vanish. Soon it swelled to an opening into a place filled with light.

The entrance was narrow, and despite a strong crosscurrent, I made it through without touching the rocks on either side. Once inside the cavern, I rose to the surface.

The sight was breathtaking—the walls and ceiling of the cave were flooded with a golden light that wavered and rippled from the reflection of the water below. Where they arched over me, teeth of stone flashed with crystals of all colors as the light struck them. This indeed was the cavern Aleea and Torvald had described.

Turning around, I saw an opening high in the wall. There were a number of these where the sun shone through at various times of day, and the wind sang through them at all times in a musical murmur. For a moment I thought that all I'd heard of the sea people's song was only this melodious wind and that I'd imagined the words. A deep sense of disappointment washed over me. "This is all foolishness," I said to myself, "and I am a fool to have followed it."

But then, unmistakably, as if they had read my thoughts, the song of the mermen and mermaids came louder and clearer than before:

> *Now, in the music that murmurs like a river*
> *Where we swim in our bright golden caverns forever,*
> *Turn about, turn about, seek the glimmering ray*
> *Where the foam flies and the conch horn plays.*

I turned once again and saw a low entrance on the surface of the water, covered and uncovered as the water rose and fell. A white shape flashed by it, and with the flip of a tail, disappeared. I cried out and swam after it.

I ducked under the low rock and swam out under a sky cerulean blue, as if freshly rinsed by rain. The water before me shone aquamarine with purple and green currents winding through it. The waves sparkled, dancing in the sun as they rolled toward the yellow sand of a little cove. Where the whitecaps broke, bits of foam flashed into the air and vanished.

The song came louder than before. Now I could hear the distinct parts, the high voices and low joining in harmony:

> *High on the wave, the sun shines brightly,*
> *Firebird winging across the sky,*
> *While under him waves come dancing lightly,*

Blue and white, green and white, they go by.
In the evening the moonbird seeks her lover—
Alone through the purple night watch her fly.

My heart leaped forward with a sharp pang of desire, so sharp I thought I was dying. The singing seemed to come from around a high spur of the cliff where the little beach ended, though from the way the sounds echoed off the cliff, I was confused.

The light appeared brighter beyond the cliff and I swam toward it. As I rounded the point, a stiff gale caught me in the face, smelling of sea and land at once. The fragrance was sharp and increased my longing.

The music swelled too, but I hardly noticed. For there on the other side, gathered upon the rocks at the back of the bay, radiant with a brightness that hurt my eyes, sang the mermen and mermaids.

It was as if my eyes were open for the first time. Everything radiated light. From the green and blue hollows of the waves, shining like gems, to the fiery radiance of the froth, to the glowing sky, light shone through all. The gray and purple cliffs reflected it in a way that brought out every feature of the rock, every crack and leaning stone in the talus, every shadow and weather-beaten surface. The crescent of sand shone like yellow topaz. And there on the rocks, almost too bright to look upon, reclined the mermen and mermaids—their tails lustrous with silver, or aquamarine, or lavender, shimmering as they twitched and moved; their skin gold or white shading to green; their hair pale, streaming down their backs, or dark, clustered in deep green curls about their shoulders.

But their faces—I can't describe their faces—for these were living light and no words can do them justice. When my eyes caught theirs, blazing like stars in the night sky—only closer—my own filled with tears and I wept with the happiness of desire. It was a desire both fulfilled and renewed as I looked upon them and listened to their ravishing music:

> You have come to us now, where land and sea marry,
> Where the heart knows its home in the hollows of waves,
> Where the sky above blends with the ocean beneath it,
> While the music rises and the music falls.

Their music was desire itself, and I realized how it could be dangerous, drawing mariners upon the rocks and leaving whales stranded near the shore to suffocate under their own weight. And yet what I mostly noticed in this light and music were small things—how the merest yellow lichen on a rock seemed to radiate a glory that was infinite, or how a white snail shell, or a bit of green seaweed curling back and forth in a tidal pool, seemed to carry the mystery of the universe in its coils. Meanwhile, the glittering flank of a merman or white arm of a mermaid appeared, in its beauty, a path to the stars.

And the look on their faces was indescribable, for the light that shone from them, or through them, was like . . . well . . . like coming home and knowing it as home for the first time.

I felt hugely content and alive in the presence of this light and singing, and for a while I lay there, letting it flood me. For their part, though they smiled at me, the mermen did not seem surprised and continued their song without interruption.

Suddenly the chorus stopped and there was absolute silence, but a silence in which the music seemed to move beyond the reaches of a mortal ear. And the light increased.

Then the leader, with hair silver as starlight, turned toward me. He was the oldest among them, though he did not seem old at all, his skin ruddy and smooth, his flukes alive and supple. Seated next to the merman was the oldest and wisest of the mermaids, with dark green hair sweeping down her back and a spray of crystals from the sea caves in it, flashing like stars. A gold light shone from her body and face. Her tail was a dark lustrous green.

At last the leader spoke: "Hralekana, we salute you. For the story of your deeds has preceded you. Each calls forth our praise and deserves honor, especially your victory over the Kraken at the center of the sea." He paused and all looked at me, their faces growing more radiant by the moment.

"We know that you are troubled, as are we, by the destruction threatening the earth, the ocean, and every plant and animal that dwells therein." Here I noticed a low chorus to his words, so low as to be almost inaudible, fading as his words turned to the plight of the earth and swelling as he spoke more hopefully.

"You know the story," he said, "of the days we lived on the shores of a large island in the center of the ocean in perfect harmony with water, land, beast, bird, and fish. And how we spent the days and nights singing with all creation under the sun and moon. How your kind, the whales—every different one—came and sang with us, together with the seals and walruses, the dolphins and birds—each according to its capacity—but how the Humpbacks were the most musical of the beasts."

I felt a wave of pride move through me.

"And how of the harsh notes of the gulls and curlews we made harmony, and even of the groaning of the Ice at the End of the World, and the seething of the fiery springs, and the moaning of the earth as rock slid over rock or volcano bellowed. Each sound was part of the music we made."

He paused with a faraway look in his eyes. He murmured, "And all creatures made one music, which ever rose up from that isle in the center of the ocean, a ceaseless fountain of praise and gratitude for everything in creation."

Then his face darkened. "But you also know how a wave came in one night and overwhelmed the island so that we were scattered to the seven corners of the seas." Here the chorus rose in a crescendo of dissonance and loud lamenting.

"Yet," he continued, "as you can see, we survived, and still live in harmony with all things, and our song ever ascends. For we honor the dumb creatures who cannot speak and live blithely in the moment, and even the least seaweed under the wave, and the rock itself. For we know that each of these simple creatures is good in its own right, and also part of us, to whom it gives great good, as the water, the simple clear creature we swim in, is part of us.

"Yet we know that water and rock and air are not as simple as they appear but are themselves made up of profound mysteries. Even more so are the plants and animals, the stars and sun and moon. And light itself. We know that the tiniest visible thing is a complex creature in its own right and contains within it worlds. The smallest bit of plankton is a universe in which many mysteries revolve.

"And, knowing this, what can we begin to say of whale, merman, or human?" For a moment there was absolute silence.

The chorus began again, swelling louder, and I heard in the different voices the humming of many energies blended together. I thought of the swirling plankton upon which the krill fed and the whirling herring and the thousand stars that turn in great spirals above us.

Now it seemed as if their music transported me, for I no longer saw them but rather moved through the universe—from the smallest, even invisible things, where I saw bits of light revolving about one another, through all creatures, rocks, and plants. Each seemed to be transparent. In each of them as it flashed before me I saw veins of crystal or blood or the green blood of plants move—and all the tiny multitudes that make up the largest, flash and turn and hum. Everywhere I saw light turn and flash, and finally I moved beyond the planet in my seeing and saw the earth flash blue and green as it turned about the sun, and our sun as a white light in a dark sky and then as one of thousands of stars turning in a spiral across the night. And everywhere I heard the hum, the music of being.

Finally, the stars appeared to flee toward a central cluster and became one solid blaze of light, tiny in the void, no larger than a scallop shell. Surrounding it, holding it up, was a vast radiant spout. Then everything vanished and the sky returned, and I was looking into the bright eyes of the merman leader.

Next his consort, the mermaid, spoke: "Like us, you do not build things, except for your music, nor destroy the waters you live in. Like us, you understand the harmony of all creatures. With man, it is different. He builds, but he also destroys. His powers are great for good or for evil. Man has been gifted with power that he chooses not to control. He brings a blight upon the earth we love.

"It has to do with the greatest of mysteries, the shadow that lurks at the edge of things." She nodded at me knowingly. "A mystery you are not ignorant of.

"And therefore, since the early days when man swam in flimsy craft upon the sea, we have watched him. Once we even swam by his side. But in recent years we have seen the horrors he has brought upon life in the ocean, and we choose not to appear to him. Once in a great while an exhausted, shipwrecked sailor floats near our shores and hears our singing—only to think he is near madness.

"Humans must learn to love the earth and the ocean and to cherish them as their own flesh, to see them as filled with the same spirit that fills themselves and all creatures. They need to listen to the music of all the worlds, to learn the harmony of creation and to live in it."

She paused and the chorus swelled in answer to her while the gale again blew strong. I knew that our meeting was over. Their voices swelled with the wind and great whitecaps rolled into the rocks, sending columns of spray rising over them to the top of the cliff. At each wave they sang louder.

I was pushed by the waves dangerously close to the rocks, so I submerged, where the singing followed me through the water:

> *Look for us now where the sea currents flow,*
> *Where the dark waters over you twist and twine*
> *Around and around till you do not know*
> *Where you are going. Lost, you suddenly find*
> *The way you are looking for. . .*

I swam through the crosscurrents and rounded the cliff to the entrance of the cave, which flashed with a golden light within. Once inside, I lingered a while, reluctant to leave. Then I headed down into the dark opening through which I'd originally entered the cavern.

Down I went, their song surrounding me, guiding me away from that mysterious place, down into the Black Deep until it was the merest whisper. The whisper followed me a long time and disappeared when I saw in the distance a bluish glow from Hralekana's cavern. I entered it once again and lay there long, thinking about what I had heard and seen.

At last I knew it was time to leave this place too, and I rose to the surface.

Chapter Seventeen

When I left the cave, for some reason I felt drawn to the Ice at the End of the World. For two days I swam into colder waters before I saw any ice. I heard it before I saw it. As spring advanced, the ice was shaking loose from the ice shelf, shuddering, cracking, and groaning its way to open sea. The huge icebergs, shining white, blue, and green as they turned from sun to shadow, revolving in mists crowned by ever-fading and shifting rainbows, made a symphony that resounded through that cold ocean.

While I swam among them, the memory of the mermen's music filled every crevice of my being, and I delighted in the contrast between it and the gigantic cacophony around me. In quiet spells among the ice, I even tried singing some of it aloud. When I did so, the seas around me took on a more intense green and white, a wildness and an emptiness that was profound. The blue and green icebergs were presences from a dream, and I swam under and around their vast hulks, sometimes rising just as one dropped a load of snow and crystals, rocking the water about me.

At sunrise and moonrise I thought I heard snatches of the mermen themselves singing. I wasn't sure, and I listened intently one whole night when the surface was a mirror reflecting the rising moon and stars. The icebergs floated over the water like giant misshapen birds hidden in a mist. I heard just a snatch of their song, at a seemingly infinite distance, and it went through me like an icy crystal.

Hearing that, I felt the keenest delight in my solitude and sang of it to the moon:

Where waters are cold and the moon is clear,
Where ice mountains rise far over the horizon,
Where salt tastes sharp and the ocean is empty,
The heart expands to the sea's brimming edge.

There was a freshness to the world as it came forth from its root, to these icebergs arriving from the interior of the Pole, that healed and filled.

The next morning I was ready to swim home to the islands, traveling by both sun and moon. I thought of the pod, especially of the twins Hvala and Lūvah preparing for their first journey to the krill. How excited they would be. I was eager to see them and swam day and night. At last the morning came when I saw three splashes on the horizon—one large and two little ones. Soon the four of us were together. We rolled, hugging and rubbing each other.

We swam slowly to the island, its mountain covered by clouds. While Aleea and I shared what had happened in my absence, Hvala and Lūvah swam in quick circles about us, chasing each other and whistling, leaping over our tails. I reached up with my flukes and caught Hvala midair, launching him over my head high into the sunlight. He arched down beautifully, and Lūvah asked for her turn. Nearly all white, she flew through the air like some sleek gull, her flippers stretched wide. Then Hvala was back, begging to be tossed again. It was noon before we came up to the rest of the pod, near the lagoon.

They were eager for news about the home of the *Rainbow Whale*, and I related what I had seen and heard. They were troubled to hear that the rivers flowed with poison and that I hadn't been able to swim far into the bay. Hrūna and Lewtë were especially concerned, recalling their own long stay in those waters. That night as we lay together, softly bumping against each other in the gentle swell, I told the pod of my visit to the mermen and mermaids and of what they showed me of the earth and all creation. While the others drifted off to sleep under a moon as fair as the queen of mermaids, I sang a little of the music I'd heard.

We spent the next morning showing the twins how to bubble net herring and capelin. This was their first taste of anything besides their mother's milk. Mostly they came up empty, but the hunt gave Aleea a chance to feed before the long journey to the Pole.

On the following day, before the sun broke the water, the pod left for the Ice at the End of World. The calves, in the center of the circle, leaped and shimmied with excitement. They jumped over each other, braiding their wakes together. I warned them to save their strength for the journey.

Several nights out, we rested near the edge of the Waste Sea and I explained to Hvala and Lūvah the bone-white sea bottom that stretched to the horizon under the moon. They stared silently as I told them about the giant fireball that years ago had eaten the island and all life in this part of the sea. After that, they were quiet a long time. I myself felt troubled and had difficulty sleeping, though I knew not why. It was a clear night and the stars shone white and large, their flippers spread. Everyone around me slept deeply. At last, watching the flukes of the Leaping Whale slip over the horizon, I drifted off into uneasy dreams.

In the morning thick fog hid the sun. We were slow to wake and get under way. We had barely started out when we heard the sound of an iron monster following us. Soon, a dark shape appeared in the fog behind us. Hrūna ordered the pod to dive while we two stayed low on the surface. I heard the *thrug thrug* of screws and the *ping* of an echo finder. A pirate whaler, perhaps, but something about the screws was familiar, and I swam toward them. In a minute the fog parted and the *Rainbow Whale* hove into view. Mark was standing on her bow. He shouted and waved. I trumpeted, leaping out of the water.

A moment later Hrūna was beside me and the others returned to the surface. The *Rainbow Whale* stopped her engines and turned broadside. I swam up to her and affectionately thumped her with my tail. Mark was at the rail in his black skin and flippers, looking worried. Without a word, he was over the side onto my back, lying with his face over my blowhole.

I was stunned by what he had to tell me, and I lay stiff in the water as the others crowded close. The news was something no one had expected. When Mark and the crew of the *Rainbow Whale* heard it in port, they'd immediately sailed in search of us. They'd sped across the ocean to the island, arriving two nights ago, only to find us gone on the spring migration. Guessing our course, they'd followed swiftly after, listening with echo finders for any sign of our presence.

The pictures rushed into my mind; I'm not sure I fully understood all of them, but I understood enough.

Mark's voice was low and somber. He showed me again how he and the *Rainbow Whale* had earlier persuaded the men on the island to put the metal egg back on a ship. This was the egg the men had planned to explode in a monstrous fireball that would eat the island and spread the Invisible Burning throughout the sea. Other ships had arrived from other pods of humans to support the *Rainbow Whale*'s protest, and it was just a matter of time before the whole fleet left the island and took the metal egg back from where it came.

During the recent full moon the warships had at last left the island and sailed for several days before a typhoon struck. They were far from any rocky shores, so the sailors were not concerned in their large ships but sailed full speed ahead into it. But, without anyone understanding how it happened, in the storm one of the iron monsters rammed the one carrying the metal egg, cutting the ship in half.

The crew from that ship were rescued before it sank, but in the confusion the metal egg slipped out and fell miles into the ocean—into the deep trench where fires seethe from the inside of the earth and liquid rock is born.

Iron whales and divers had gone down to search for it, but it lay too deep for them. And the metal egg was even too far down for the small iron whale that could go deepest of all. The danger lay in the pressure at that great depth.

The pictures that passed through my mind as Mark spoke were now more difficult to make sense of. They were pictures of what might happen. I saw two different metals inside the metal egg, both of which gave off the Invisible Burning, deadly to creatures. If the shell of the metal egg cracked, the two metals could be driven together and create a giant explosion, a fireball that would tear up the ocean floor and make the water deadly with the Invisible Burning for miles around. In turn, the deadly water would move throughout the ocean. No one knew how far the Invisible Burning would spread, but it might reach all the waters around the earth.

No human knew for sure how deadly the Invisible Burning might be in the end, but it was far more deadly than that in the fireball that created the Waste Sea. It could possibly kill all life in the ocean. Without life in the ocean, life on land would die.

Mark fell silent, and after I passed on what he'd shown me, the pod lay silent. Even the calves lay quietly in the water, staring wide-eyed at the adults. The only sound was the ringing of waves against the hull of the *Rainbow Whale*.

Far in the distance a sea gull began to cry. Urgently mewing, it crossed above us and flew west, disappearing over the horizon. I felt water from Mark's eyes fall down my blowhole. And, before he could tell me, I knew why he was grieving.

"Hralekana," he murmured and paused. "Hralekana . . ." and his voice failed. There was no sound but the ringing of the waves. But the pictures came clear in my head. I saw myself descend into the trench and take up the metal egg in my mouth, swollen huge from its size. I saw myself lift it a long way up to the little iron whale. The iron whale took the egg from me and carried it up to the ships. But I also saw another possible picture: I saw myself drop the egg and a bright flash rise from the Deep.

"I understand, Mark. They want me to bring up the metal egg," I said, my voice flat, overwhelmed by the thought.

"The danger is very great," Mark squeezed out the words. "Moving it could cause it to . . ." His voice faded, and again I saw what he meant.

"Explode," I said. "If it did, the danger to us all would be great."

Hvala and Lūvah, who had been listening, their noses pressed close to my right eye, whimpered when I said "explode." Aleea took them away.

"It might be too heavy for you, and in that case you would leave it," Mark said. Then his voice rose and I could feel the anger in it. "The fools! Why did they build it and take it to the ocean in the first place? Oh, Hralekana, I am sorry for my kind. . . ." He struck his belly with his flipper.

"Anyone would understand—" his voice grew calmer— "everyone would understand if you did not go down after the egg.

200

No one would blame you." From the tone of his voice, I knew he hoped I would refuse. Part of him hoped that, but another part knew he had to ask me.

My heart felt a weight descend upon it, pulling it down, a weight as heavy as the anchors in the Ships' Graveyard. I knew already what my answer would be, knew from my Seeings in the Fiery Trench long ago, and from what the Whale of Light had showed me in the cavern.

"I will go," I said. "I will do my best to lift the metal egg from the ocean floor."

For a moment my words hung in the silent air. Then a high, sharp keening began. It was Aleea's, who'd returned from taking the calves out of earshot. Others joined her, including Meg, who was standing above us on the rail. Mark lay down again and said no more.

The keening went on, and I didn't have the heart to stop it.

Gradually the keening died down. In the silence, I thought of what I must do, and the thoughts were not reassuring. Even if I were able to lift the metal egg from the bottom and deliver it to the men, the Invisible Burning from inside it—the same I had felt in the presence of the iron whales—could harm me. To hold that Invisible Burning in my mouth, even for a short time, might prove fatal. As for the possibility of its exploding—I couldn't bear to think of that. I put it from my mind.

My one positive thought was that at least the pod would be far from me and the metal egg. Hrūna called the Council of Elders, and it was quickly agreed that the pod should journey on to the Ice at the End of the World to find the krill beds. According to the scouts sent earlier, these had grown rapidly in the past year and were nearly half their former size. If the metal egg exploded, the pod, of course, would have to abandon the krill and flee to the other side of the Pole. Until then, however, the nursing mothers and the rest could feed.

The *Rainbow Whale* would guide me to where the fleet was, marking the spot the metal egg had sunk. I was relieved the others would be safely far away and protested when Hrūna ruled that he, Lewtë, and Aleea would accompany me to where I must dive.

"There is no need for that," I said. "Besides, someone must stay with the twins." I looked at Aleea, but she gave me a look that meant her mind was made up. A friend of hers, a nursing mother, said gently: "Hvala and Lūvah will do well with me, for they are nearly weaned and will soon be eating krill."

Then Hrūna spoke gravely. "It is the very least we can do. You will still go on the most dangerous part of the journey alone."

I protested again, but in vain.

Leaving Hvala and Lūvah was one of the most difficult things I'd ever done. We comforted them that night, rocking on the waves under a moon swelling toward the full. Softly Aleea sang to them the old lullaby,

> Around, over, and under the sea,
> Come, O come, white whale to me . . .

until their steady breathing filled the sweet night air. Then she and I pressed close to each other, but neither of us slept.

Chapter Eighteen

In the morning the rest of the pod left for the krill beds. Before they left, Aleea and I held Hvala and Lūvah between us, crooning to them. Then, with Hrūna and Lewtë, we lay watching the pod's spouts fade over the horizon, especially those smaller ones in the center of the circle. Just before they disappeared we saw two tiny white and black shapes leap high together, their spray silver in the rising sun.

The *Rainbow Whale* coughed and vibrated in the water and started off slowly to the west. With heavy hearts we followed, each of us alone with his thoughts. Clouds gathered in the west and a cold wind rushed over the water that day and the next. At night the *Rainbow Whale* cast anchor, her eyes burning red and green on either side and white at her nose and tail. We lay close to her hull and Mark spent the night on deck. The three of us spoke far into the night.

I cannot recall all that was shared on that night or the following ones, but we knew at the time those nights were a gift we would never forget.

When Mark fell asleep, Aleea and I swam off under a half moon over which dark clouds blew in shreds. What passed between us then only the two of us will ever know. Out of our weakness we somehow gave each other strength.

In a few days, when the sun was setting, black shapes appeared over the horizon. Soon their forms were unmistakable against the sullen clouds and blood-red disk of the sun. I recognized the lean, shark noses of the warships that had been anchored at the island the year before. The same sense of uneasiness came over me.

Clouds folded over the setting sun and soon all the world was as gray as the ships, which faded into the dark as their eyes blinked open. One of the eyes winked several times at us, and the *Rainbow Whale* winked back—a signal, as Mark explained. The *Rainbow Whale* dropped anchor, and we spent the night huddled together not far from the gray ships, smelling the burnt oil they left in the water. Throughout the night they clanged, vibrated, and hummed as men moved about inside them. The ships constantly sucked in water and spewed it out again, foul. I slept fitfully. Aleea and Lewtë did not sleep at all, nor did Mark, who stood silently on the prow or paced the deck when not speaking with one of us.

I woke during the false dawn and watched the warships take shape in the gray light. Mark was staring at the ships through black tubes pressed to his eyes. Again one of the ships' eyes winked. Mark said a small boat would come soon to lead me to a point directly over the metal egg lying miles below on the ocean floor.

I swam over to Hrūna and Lewtë to say good-bye. Few words passed between us, for everything that could be, had been said in the past few days. Both pressed me between their flippers for a long time.

Then Aleea and I swam off a little way, lying side to side. Again, words were unnecessary; our thoughts were one. The whole of our lives together unwound through our minds, from our first meeting in the lagoon long ago, through the weaving of our breaths together and the dangers we had passed, to the birth of Hvala and Lūvah. All passed before us and then we simply lay there, our minds empty except of each other, as the gray sky brightened to blue.

A cry rang from the *Rainbow Whale* and I glanced over at the fleet. A white boat had left one of the larger ships and was speeding toward us. I nuzzled Aleea and for a moment we gazed at each other eye to eye. Then I turned away toward the *Rainbow Whale*, where Mark was climbing over the side ready to jump into the small boat.

It moved out from the yellow ship's side and waited, vibrating in the water while I swam up to it. Mark knelt on its nose and climbed onto my back. He lay down by my blowhole, motioning for me to follow the boat.

The boat moved slowly and I followed. Mark was silent. We steered a course between the warships and on the far side saw a yellow buoy marking the spot. The sun had risen by now and the buoy gleamed brightly. The boat turned to one side and a man in the stern pointed to it.

I looked back and saw that Hrūna, Lewtë, and Aleea had followed, their skin gleaming in the morning sun.

Mark was trying to say something, but the words wouldn't come. It didn't matter, since I saw the picture clearly in my mind—of him standing on the shore waving good-bye after Aleea and I escaped from the tidal basin long ago. I knew what he was thinking: that neither of us should fear, for we would meet again.

I slipped alongside the boat and Mark climbed into it. Swimming up to the yellow buoy and breathing deeply, I sang my battle song into that bright morning:

> Now I go to battle, my breath's banner
> Bright to behold in the height of the morning.
> Hralekana-kolua on the crest of the comber
> Lifts up his cry to creation's four corners.

I trumpeted loudly and, looking toward Mark, sang in a softer tone:

> *Wherever on the waters the winds shall find you,*
> *Wherever the moon or the sun shall move,*
> *Hidden in the heavens or splendid high above you,*
> *Deep in my heart I will breathe deeply with you*
> *The breath of the one who made you and keeps you.*

Finally, gazing back into the sun toward Aleea, I sang to her:

> *Surely as the sun swims after the moon,*
> *So does my heart press hard after yours.*
> *Though my flukes fly as far as the Pole,*
> *My soul sails to you as if to its center.*

Sucking in a last deep breath, I dove, smacking the surface with my flukes one last time.

Down through the Green Deep I swam, into the Blue—straight down, but not too quickly, in order to save my strength. Aleea, Hrūna, and Lewtë dove too and were soon alongside me. Silently we descended together to the edge of the Black Deep, where a small iron whale, brightly colored and with shining eyes, churned up to us. It was to guide me part of the way down through the Black Deep—though I did not need a guide.

Aleea and I pressed against each other. I stroked her with my flipper and we looked one last time into each other's eyes. Then I headed down till the whales were three small silhouettes against the fading surface. Soon the water was dark above, and only the bright light from the iron whale made a small circle in the black void.

The water was growing colder and far below I saw pinpoints of light—the transparent electric fish I'd met before in the deep, swimming in strange galaxies and giving off their own light. They clustered around the iron whale as we passed through them, attracted by its lights, for it resembled a giant electric fish.

Soon the fish faded above us, turning like stars in the sky. I felt the dark close on me like a giant mouth. By now the pressure was familiar. I recalled earlier dives: the one down to the giant ship in the other ocean, my dive there to the Fiery Trench, as well as my dive into the pit where the Kraken lay.

To my right the little iron whale whirred its way down, but soon with three short whistles it signaled it could go no deeper. I whistled back, and it waggled its stiff flippers and blinked its eyes, opening and closing the large lobsterlike claw that stuck out from its nose. This was to remind me that it would take the metal egg from me when I lifted it from the bottom. Then with a whirr the iron whale rose toward the surface.

I watched its three eyes shrink to points in the blackness. They vanished entirely and I was alone in the dark, which pressed close to me now like a familiar friend—a cold friend, but I was growing numb to the cold. Down I swam, emitting short whistles to bounce off the bottom, still far away. By the echoes I kept myself on a perpendicular descent. The pressure grew, as did the cold, and from a compressed corner of my mind the thought came that I might be crushed before reaching the bottom.

My eyes felt pushed back into my head and my flippers felt smaller. Both flippers and flukes stiffened with the cold. For periods of time my mind went blank, and I worried that the cold was numbing it. This must be what it was like to freeze to death, I thought. Then for a moment I was sure I was hallucinating. I heard whispers. Listening closely, I realized Aleea, Lewtë, and

Hrūna were singing on the surface far above. I could make out the music, but no words, and I focused on listening to it as I descended, keeping my mind clear that way. I moved my flippers rapidly, trying to warm myself as I pulled downward, thrusting with what strength I had.

Their song went on for a long time. It seemed as if hours had passed since I left their company. The deeper the water, the colder, and my one thought beside the music was the next stroke of my flippers. Gradually, however, the water seemed warmer. I thought it must be the false warmth felt by those about to die from the cold.

I moved faster, trying to get as far down as possible before passing out—if that was what was going to happen. The water felt even warmer, a hint warmer. Then I saw the shadow of my flipper in the dark; and soon it shone a dim white. I could feel the blood move through my flippers now—slowly, very slowly, since my pulse had dropped to conserve air.

I caught a glimpse of something lighter in the distance, something almost white that advanced and retreated. I swam toward it and cried out in surprise. A wall of bubbles rose in front of me and stretched to either side as far as I could see. Downward, too, the wavering wall stretched out of sight.

On impulse I plunged into the wall. The bubbles burst all over me, tingling. They lifted me a few fathoms as I rolled, savoring them, and swam out before losing my direction. I felt refreshed and started down again, moving parallel to the wall.

The wall of bubbles was a source of light down there and I could see a fair distance by it. It wasn't long before I noticed something far below gleaming dully, like a pale moon. With a sharp thrill I recognized the object on the bottom. I thrust down toward it as hard as I could. The pressure was painful now but I hardly noticed. The moonlike object—the metal egg—grew larger. I fixed my eye on it as I descended. Soon it was just a few fathoms below and a voice in me cried out to stop. I felt something coming from the metal egg: the Invisible Burning. I remembered the Invisible Burning from the large iron whale that had pursued me long ago.

Mastering the panic I felt, I eased slowly down, fathom by fathom, as the metal egg swelled in size.

At last I was beside it, my flippers stirring clouds of sediment on the bottom. It was large, oval in shape, and had broken free from whatever held it. I glanced around in the dim light from the bubble wall and saw two other shapes not far off—the two halves of the ship that had carried it. One was on end, the other turned upside down. My head ached from the pressure.

The bubbles rushed from a crack in the ocean floor, but there was no sign here of the fire that bubbled and seethed from the Springs of Fire on the planet's far side. I knew though that elsewhere in this sea canyon, fire and molten rock spilled from the earth's insides. I shuddered as I thought of it.

I hesitated to begin what I'd come to do. The metal egg was large, and I was afraid it would prove too heavy. I knew that the little iron whale was waiting above, with its echo finder fixed on this egg, and probably on me too, waiting to learn if I could lift it. I knew that on the surface the larger ships also had a fix on the egg and had followed me down with their echo finders.

I recalled my vision of white flame in the Fiery Trench, and I was afraid.

But then somewhere inside, part of me asked, "What are you waiting for? If you want to get out of here, lift the egg."

Gingerly at first, I opened my mouth wide and tried to spread it around the egg, but I couldn't get my jaw under it. The egg was lodged firmly in the muck of the ocean floor. I pressed hard and my jaw hurt. The sediment swirled up around my face, blinding me, and I backed off. When it settled, I tried again, this time taking a little more of the metal egg in my mouth. But I felt a sharp twinge in my lower lip and backed off. It was bleeding.

After resting, I tried once more, and ground my jaw into the sediment. Suddenly I felt the egg shift its weight. For a moment it balanced on my lip and then rolled slowly into my mouth, filling it. I choked and started to swim upward too fast. The weight of the egg sagged, pouching out my lower jaw. I felt a wrenching pain, and the metal egg pulled me back to the bottom. I rested a moment and then tried to lift it again slowly.

With much thrusting of flukes and flippers, I managed to lift it off the bottom a fathom or two. Progress was agonizingly slow. Stroke by stroke, fathom by fathom, I climbed upward, but I wondered how long my strength would last. The ache in my head was nothing compared to that in my jaw. Every second seemed a minute, every minute an hour. I knew I couldn't make it without help. I struggled over to the bubble wall and pushed inside. The buoyancy of the bubbles helped some and distracted me from the pain. But the upward swim was slow and laborious. Hours later, it seemed, I came to the top of the bubble wall. There the bubbles thinned out and no longer helped. The water was colder and grew bitterly cold. My strength was running out.

Nevertheless, I strained upward. Once more I heard the whisper from above, the singing of the others. Somehow they knew I had the metal egg in my mouth and sang to encourage me. Yet I was beginning to see strange spots in my eyes and my mind wandered. A long time passed when I didn't know whether I was climbing or sinking. At last, far above me I heard a whistle and saw a pinpoint of light. It was the light on the small iron whale.

For a moment I felt hope. I kept my eye on the light, but the spots returned and suddenly I felt weak and dizzy. I blacked out for an instant and came to upside down. Helplessly I felt the metal egg slip from my mouth.

I thrust with my flukes, plunging down after it, terrified it would strike the bottom and burst. Though I dropped fast, the silver egg fell faster, plummeting toward the bottom. I pushed harder with my flukes and dove faster than was safe. I gained a little on the egg and, throwing caution aside, plunged with all my might. By now I was beside the curtain of bubbles and could see the ocean floor. Heaving my flukes, I was beside the egg, then under it. Opening my mouth, I caught it, but the momentum of it dragged me toward the bottom. Wildly I flailed, pushing up-ward, flipping over and nearly dropping the egg again.

Grimly I held on and slowed it, but not enough. With a jolt, we struck bottom, raising a cloud of muck. I lay stiff, afraid to move, waiting for the egg to explode. At last I tried lifting it again. The effort squeezed tears from my eyes. Slowly, painfully, I moved up one fathom, then two, before my vision clouded. I saw spots and a thread of blood unspooling from my injured lip. I paused and the egg pulled me back down.

Again I tried, and again. It was no use. The best I could do was lift the metal egg a fathom and carry it just above the ocean floor. Even at that, the old wound in my side began to throb. With the ache in my jaw and head, I was a network of pain.

I did not have the strength to lift the egg to the little iron whale. Nor would resting at the bottom increase my strength.

And who knew how much longer the metal egg could withstand the pressure of the Deep?

Still, I tried one last time to struggle up from the ocean floor. I made a little headway before the pain caused me nearly to black out. My strength was gone. Listlessly, I drifted to the bottom.

I had failed.

Chapter Nineteen

I lay there trying to force from my mind the feeling of dreadful failure. I needed to focus on what was—to think what to do next—and the feeling didn't help.

Mark had spoken of this possibility. He and the others had explained what to do if the egg proved too heavy for me to bring to the surface. I was to carry it as best I could along the trench, seeking the fiery cracks in the earth's skin. I was to find a wide crack and drop the egg into its center.

I lay there thinking of that and thinking of the danger, not just to me but to all life in this world. Mark had stressed the danger of it, that this course was to be pursued only as a last resort. The danger was that the heat would cause the metal egg to explode. (I recalled how his voice broke once while describing it.) That was why I had to drop the egg where it would fall quickly into the heart of the fire—fall in deep before the increasing heat stirred up the metals inside its shell. If the egg fell in quickly enough, the fire would destroy the shell and the metals before they could mingle. Our only hope was in the quick fiery destruction of what was itself a thing of fire.

Mark said very wise humans disagreed among themselves whether this solution would work. They all agreed that at the least there would probably be a small explosion, that the trigger for the metals to mingle was too sensitive to stand much heat and would go off. The trick was for the molten fire to destroy the metal egg in the fraction of time between the trigger's going off and the metals mingling in a gigantic explosion. Mark said that it

217

was most important for me to get as close as I could to the heart of the fire before dropping the egg, and then to turn and flee for my life.

Fortunately, the fiery cracks were in a deeper part of the trench. I did not need to climb higher with the egg, but only stay above the twisting floor of the ocean trench as it descended toward the fire. The journey was a long one, Mark had said, but except for some small ridges crossing the trench floor, all on a downward slope.

My course lay through the bubble wall. Slowly I glided forward, my mouth swollen like that of a whale scooping in a meal of krill. I entered the bubbles and immediately felt soothed by the warm tingling that moved across my skin. Almost all of the pain in my lip disappeared and the wound in my side stopped throbbing. Yet, the ache in my jaw remained. I was beginning to think the bubbles would last all the way to the fiery cracks when they vanished. I had swum out the other side.

Then I heard a sharp whistle far above me. It was a signal from the iron whale, letting me know it was tracking me toward the cracks of fire. I knew that the warships, as well as the whales, were tracking me from the surface. That made me feel a little less lonely as I moved along the dark pit.

I swam through the darkness, ever downward, and the effects of the bubble wall wore off. My jaw ached, my lip stung, and the wound in my side throbbed again. But it was the weary weight of the metal egg that bothered me most, that and the feeling of the Invisible Burning coming from it. They drained me, however slowly, of strength. I steered by echo, but with the bulbous metal egg in my mouth, my hearing wasn't as sharp as it should be, and now and then I scraped against the rocks that rose in the way.

What I feared most was smashing into one in the dark and the shock exploding the metal egg.

Now and then I'd find bubbles streaming up from a crack in the earth and, no matter how thin the stream, I moved aside into it, letting the bubbles play over my injured skin. Then it was back into the dark again, straining to catch the echoes that warned of imminent collision. At long intervals I heard a faint whistle from the little iron whale, and now and then a whisper that could be Hrūna, Lewtë, and Aleea singing.

In that dark I lost all sense of time. I couldn't tell whether hours passed or days. All I knew was that the egg grew heavier and seemed to swell in size as I carried it in my mouth, pushing slowly with my flukes. More and more often I paused, resting on the bottom. Each time it was harder to start again. In the words of one of our ancient singers,

> There passed a weary time. Each fluke
> Was sore, and glazed each eye.
> A weary time! A weary time!
> How glazed each weary eye... .

So it went for days—how many I do not know. I felt I was a permanent creature of the night, some bulbous monstrosity of the deep, a bottom crawler like the shadows that passed me. These dark shadows, which I more felt by the currents they made than actually saw, wriggled or swerved around me or regarded me with dark malice from holes in the rock. And whenever I rested on the bottom, hagfish rose out of the muck to investigate whether I was settling in for good, nipping me to see if I was alive.

Despite the horrors lurking in the rocks around me or in the mud under me, I was too weary to feel fear. Hour after hour, through an endless night, I swam downward, mustering what little strength I had to climb over low ridges in the ocean floor. The long dark and the weariness began to affect my mind, and I had to ignore strange, sometimes monstrous, visions that rose up in the void. Once I saw a ghostly tentacle writhe before me. It grew until, passing a rock, a wraithlike image of the Kraken swelled over me with its huge, unblinking eye. A corrosive whisper snaked through my head:

"You are nothing more than the muck you swim over—food for hagfish. Sleep . . . sleep on the bottom. I shall feast on you yet." Its pale eye swelled until I was swimming into it. I closed my eyes, shook my head, and the ghastly vision was gone, but I heard its horrible laugh trail after me like the chuckle of bones. After that the dark was a relief.

Still another time when I stopped to rest, I must have fallen asleep. I woke and ahead of me in the blackness a shadow moved. I lifted up my burden and followed. From then on until I reached the fiery cracks I had the sense of something swimming ahead of me just beyond my vision. When I paused, it paused, but I never caught up with it.

In my most weary moments I found that saying the one word over and over focused my thoughts away from the weariness. At other times I sang to myself a line or two of an old song. Either way, the simple repetition soothed me and kept me going.

There came a time when the darkness in front of me grew a shade lighter. It lightened until it shone faintly red. The water felt warmer and my heart quickened, knowing I was approaching the fiery cracks in the earth. Soon I could make out the shape of the ocean floor ahead of me, outlined black against the red. In the waxing and waning of the fiery light, I saw in the distance the walls of the sea canyon rise up beyond sight, forming the deep trench down which I swam.

I rested once more before the crest, then struggled to the top. Before me lay a brilliant and frightening sight. At the bottom of the slope, the skin of the earth opened and extended as far as the eye could see in a broken, zigzag line of molten red lava that boiled and seethed. From the crack shot up jets of gold and blue flame, and steam rose in a storm of bubbles writhing blue, red, and yellow as the burning gases lit them from below. The lava bubbled over and brightened to gold before being quenched by the water and sending up clouds and curtains of more steam. The fires flared and dimmed as the clouds writhed over them.

So fantastic a display of light and molten rock it was, that I lay there lost in it, my mind running to song. After a long time the pain in my jaw called me back from the spectacle and I was once more aware of the heavy object pressing my pouch to the ocean floor. I felt weak and much smaller than the inert egg anchoring me there. With a kind of dull horror I realized I must lift it and swim through those clouds of exploding gases into the heart of the fire.

I had rehearsed this moment with Mark, who'd warned me what I would find. And I had gone over it a thousand times while swimming through the Deep. I knew I must now swim as high as I could lift the metal egg and carry it to where the bubbles of steam wavered up hundreds of fathoms, reflecting in their twisting dance the red lava and blue and gold gases burning below. I must follow the crooked line of the molten crack, staying high enough to avoid the worst of the heat, to where it broadened to its widest point.

There, with less chance of the metal egg's going astray, I was to plunge toward the white heart of the fire as fast as I could and, not until the heat became unbearable, release the egg toward the white-hot depths. If I was lucky, and Mark had stressed this point—if I plunged fast enough, my momentum would propel the egg into the heart of the fire before it could explode. The egg would melt before it exploded, or if it did explode, the blast would be a small one, not the giant one that ate the ocean.

From above I heard a series of faint signals indicating the ships were moving back outside the range of either explosion.

I felt alone and helpless.

It all seemed foolish now, for my strength was at an end. My jaw and my head ached from the strain of carrying the metal egg. My skinned lips felt as if they were on fire and my old wound throbbed through the rest of my body. I'd be lucky, I thought, if I didn't tumble helplessly with the egg into the narrow red crack that opened at the bottom of the ridge.

I closed my eyes and rested a moment, summoning whatever strength remained from the depths of my being. I realized, too, that whatever happened, I had brought the egg this far and it wasn't much farther to the crack. So, resisting the grim picture of myself tumbling end over end into the abyss of flame, I gathered strength and with a lurch lifted the monstrous egg off the bottom.

The weight pulled me down the slope of the ridge. Fighting gravity, I thrust with flukes and flippers, barely angling upward. The bleeding from my lips obscured my vision. But I did gain a little height, before gravity pulled me again toward the red crack, and I flailed up again. By fits and starts I managed to keep a more or less level course over the abyss. But the crack was widening and growing hotter. Worse, I was beginning to feel delirious.

With a last surge of strength I swam into the wall of steam and gases and felt myself buoyed up, however slightly. Though it was hard to tell up from down in that rolling cloud, I climbed slowly higher. The bubbles felt cool and cleared the blood from my eyes. I climbed a score of fathoms before the weight dragged me toward the deep once again.

I could go no higher, but I kept on a level course. The difficulty now was getting a clear view of the crack below. The brilliant gases flared about and below me, creating a rainbow of eerie colors—gold, orange, violet, and green—among the bubbles. I thought of the colorful anemones and hovering clouds of jellyfish in the world above and how strange that all that beauty was here too, in the midst of destruction.

I swam out of the bubbles into an open space high above the fiery crack. Below me it gaped wide, so wide that the lava in the middle burned almost white. The heat it threw out was intense. I could barely look at the brilliant center, which rose toward me and receded as the earth spewed its molten blood, heaving up waves, sparks, and tongues of lava, creating a wall of steam that swirled around me on all sides. And I was afraid.

I was alone, helpless, and very much afraid. A thought came like cool water on blistered skin: Who was I to contend with such primal forces of the earth? I had come as far as I could, to the end of my strength, and could go no farther. If I failed to finish the mission, I had made an honorable try. Surely no one would blame me if I backed away now.

Then I thought of the others at the top, waiting—Aleea and Hrūna and Lewtë, and Mark and the crew of the *Rainbow Whale*, all counting on me. I thought of the twins starving when the Invisible Burning destroyed their krill. And I set my jaw and turned back toward the fire.

Even as I did, the walls of steam moved toward one another and I knew I must act or wait for another break. My mouth ached, and I could not hold the egg much longer. I stared again into that seething center and felt the heat from it. I tried to swim down but nothing happened. I couldn't make my muscles bend toward it. I swam in a circle and forced myself to look down again.

Something strange appeared. It may have been an hallucination, or a trick of the burning gases reflecting my shadow, but in the midst of the fire appeared the flaming outline of a whale, brighter than the fire itself. At that sight I lost my fear; rather, my fear no longer mattered. Letting the weight pull me, I aimed straight down and with a thrust of my flukes sped toward the burning maelstrom. Faster and faster I dove, and the roaring heat of the crack opened like a mouth to sear me. I was blistering on all sides, but I pushed harder, blinded by the brilliance of that sea and the fiery leviathan that beckoned.

For a moment I didn't care that I would be burned, and I felt a strange freedom looking down at that shape swimming in fire. I imagined myself dissolving—my skin, flukes, and flippers disappearing, as in my vision at the Springs of Fire. Then the shock of the heat seared my whole mouth. Another moment and it would be too late.

I opened my mouth. The egg flew from my lower jaw. For a moment I saw its shape black against the flame; it shrank, speeding down into the molten heart. My flippers flashed like flames as I spread them and bent toward the surface, thrusting up with my flukes, which felt on fire behind me.

My lungs were on fire too, but without the weight in my mouth, I felt a surge of power and I thrust up into the space between the bubble walls. Only a few seconds passed, but I was fathoms higher and veered to enter the wall, knowing it would help lift me away from danger.

And then above me the bubbles lit a brilliant white, and I knew, before I felt anything, that the metal egg had exploded.

The next instant fire ate my tail and moved through me in a single searing pain.

My eyes saw nothing but fire, a brilliant white light. I felt no pain now but felt myself expanding. It was as if my skin did not exist and I was the fire—I was the light expanding into light and as I moved upward and outward the light grew brighter.

Then the light was the sky seen through the surface, and I was rapidly moving toward it. Soon—I don't know how, but somehow—I was above the water looking down, and I could see everything clearly.

I saw the ships below me and the little yellow ship with Mark and the others at the railing, and beside them the familiar shapes of Aleea, Hrūna, and Lewtë gathered near the bow. I saw everything minutely, from the sea lice and barnacles on Hrūna's back to the grieving look on Aleea's face. They were all staring at the water where it was heaving up, a white boiling eye on the green ocean, sending forth giant ripples as a rumbling shook the Deep.

While I watched, large waves surged from the foaming center and Aleea and my parents rose up and sank down, and even the warships miles away rocked like buoys. After the waves passed, the waters grew more calm, though the center still boiled with foam. Aleea and the others watched the foam intently, waiting for something.

Then I rose high above that ocean until I saw beyond the bend of the horizon—saw land far off, and mountains, and the glittering cities of humans. I rose above the clouds and all was light again. I moved very swiftly into the light—like a long corridor of sunlight in the sea through which I was swimming toward a brightness at the end.

And then everything changed and I had Seeings, more Seeings than ever before, but they were connected to all those that came before and to everything that had happened in my life. I saw it all clearly, as if in one picture. I saw things that I cannot describe, for there are no words for them—and things that I am not permitted to tell. And I uttered my word, and it sprang from my mouth like a flaming bird, an albatross of fire, and flew up into that light. And the light answered.

The next thing I knew I was over the ocean again and the ships had all moved in toward the center, which had ceased rocking and foaming. Ahead of them Aleea, Hrūna, and Lewtë were swimming, each in a different direction, as if looking for something.

I was descending fast, the waters wrinkling green and white below. Then I was under them and moving down into the Blue Deep toward the Black. Just at the edge of the Black Deep I saw something white rise toward me, end over end, nose over flukes, flippers extending stiffly from its sides. It shocked me to see it. Its eyes were squeezed shut and its hide blistered and torn. While I watched, it grew larger, looming before me. My vision swam, all went dark, and I remembered no more.

Chapter Twenty

I, Hrūna, father of Hralekana, tell now of what passed after my son left us. May his great deed be ever blessed and celebrated in the memory of the whales and all the peoples of the ocean!

The sadness of our parting can hardly be expressed. For we knew there was little chance that we would ever see him again alive. His mother Lewtë and I held back our grief and lay in silence while Hralekana parted from his mate Aleea, the mother of his twins, Hvala and Lūvah. Then we three followed him down to the Black Deep and watched him vanish into it, our hearts sinking with him. As he disappeared below, we sang to him to keep up his courage and our own.

We returned to the top, comforting Aleea in her tears. Mark waited silently in the rubber raft nearby. Now and then we forced ourselves to sing. Hours passed, and then the first day.

That first night was cold and comfortless, but we cheered ourselves with the hope that Hralekana would raise the metal egg from the floor of the sea canyon. The stars shone and the bright flukes of the Leaping Whale were reflected on the water.

The next morning the echoes told us Hralekana was rising from the Deep, slowly bearing a great weight, and our hearts rose with him. All that morning we hardly dared speak to one another but sang encouragement through the water. Then there came the terrible moment when we felt him hesitate, and afterward tracked two things moving swiftly toward the bottom. We knew, even before the signal from the iron whale, that Hralekana had dropped the metal egg. It was too heavy for him. The ships moved swiftly away to a safe distance in case the egg should explode, but we forgot to follow.

Later we sensed movement on the bottom. The iron whale signaled that Hralekana had retrieved the metal egg and was carrying it along the canyon floor. It was then we lost almost all hope. We knew the danger of the second plan—that Hralekana was likely to be destroyed in the fiery crack with the metal egg he carried to it. From that point on, we hardly dared look at one another, our hearts were so heavy.

We swam slowly forward, staying above him, always ahead of the *Rainbow Whale* and the other ships that followed farther off. Our hearts felt as heavy as the metal egg in Hralekana's mouth and, if we let them, would have dragged us down into that black abyss.

Days passed, and we moved slowly and didn't speak. Mark was always in the rubber raft or on the nose of the *Rainbow Whale*. He even slept on deck. The next day was gray with clouds again, and time dragged by. The following morning was still dark when the signal came from the iron whale that Hralekana had reached the fiery cracks within the trench and that we and the fleet should move back. Reluctantly, we turned and swam toward a red dawn opening like a wound in the sky. None of us could utter a word.

At last we turned around and gazed west in silence, hardly daring to breathe. Nothing happened. For a long while we lay there, and hope was beginning to return to us. We had just begun to breathe more easily when what we dreaded most occurred.

The water below us lit up. There was a bright flash and a few seconds later the ocean shook with a rumble that came in waves, vibrating through the Deep and shaking us from nose to flukes. Aleea gave out a thin, desperate cry and Lewtë moaned.

A moment later the water in front of us rose in a dome and collapsed, and a large wave rushed toward us. We lay stunned as it rushed down upon us, lifting us up and over its high crest. It was followed by another and another. The rumbling from below ceased, and the waves came smaller and smaller until all that remained on the surface was foam and currents moving this way and that.

We swam forward, our hearts in our throats, staring at every patch of white foam and listening, afraid of both what we might find and what we might not. We didn't care what danger lurked in that water from the Invisible Burning Mark had described. We were looking for Hralekana.

Behind us the *thrug thrug* of the *Rainbow Whale* started up and the distant roar of the warships as they prepared to return now that it was safe. We crisscrossed the area, but found nothing— nothing more came up from that terrible Deep. In dread we looked at each other, hollow-eyed.

Everything grew still. The ships behind us paused, and the water barely rippled. The dawn brightened behind us and to the west one small cloud glowed pink, as if nothing had happened. While the light leveled its beams over the water, we crisscrossed the spot again. The water was mirrorlike, yet we could see nothing in its black depths.

Then I thought I saw something dimly white move far below. It was rising slowly. At last, as the sun climbed over the ocean rim, something bobbed above the surface, rose white and stiff out of the water with flippers extending rigid from its sides, paused, and fell over like a tree in a storm.

Aleea and Lewtë cried out, and in an instant we were at Hralekana's side, where he lay stiff, eyes shut. His body was battered and lacerated. There were bloody cuts on his lips, belly, and flukes, and his skin was scraped raw. The old wound in the side was visible. But no blood flowed. When all three of us pressed against him, he felt cold—as cold as the water about him. His white skin was drab. The radiance of the living Hralekana was gone.

The high keening of the Humpbacks' lament rose sharply above me. For a long time we lay there pressed against Hralekana while the ancient wordless song of grief resounded through water and air.

We heard the soft *thrug thrug* of the *Rainbow Whale* come up behind us, but we paid no attention to her. I felt something soft bump against me and heard short choking noises. I opened one eye to see Mark beside me in a rubber raft, keening in the strange way humans do.

He climbed on Aleea's back for a few minutes, and then onto my back. I felt the water from his face trickle down my blowhole. At last, between spells of keening, he uttered sounds and I saw in my mind the pictures of what he meant. The first picture showed me that Hralekana's mission had succeeded. The metal egg had fallen into the fiery crack before it could eat the ocean. There had been an explosion, but not the enormous one all feared. The small explosion that was to trigger the large one had gone off, but the metal egg had melted before the second one could happen. There was no Invisible Burning in the water.

I knew that was something to be thankful for, but my heart was too heavy. Even when Mark told me that the black box had heard that all humans on earth had agreed to stop exploding metal eggs in the ocean, the news made little impression. My son lay cold and lifeless on the waves.

While they keened, Aleea and Lewtë stroked his body, wiping away the blood where it had dried on belly, sides, and lips. The countless small wounds and scrapes, together with the old wound in his side, were still visible when they were done—smaller, but in sharp contrast to his pale skin. When they finished, the three of us turned the body right side up. All grew silent. For a long while we lay staring at Halekana as the waves lapped against his sides.

At last, singing a dirge, Aleea and Lewtë pushed against his head and pointed him toward the Pole. Mark returned to the raft and I swam underneath Hralekana. The three of us carried him slowly, beginning the long journey to the cold waters while our traditional dirge resonated through the Deep:

Gone is he from the great sea, gone from the restless waters,
Hralekana the keen warrior, comfort of an aging heart. . . .

Behind us came the raft with Mark and two of the crew. Behind this crept the yellow ship herself, and behind her, the gray ships followed. The procession had moved slowly along for several hours when a number of explosions from the gray ships shook the ocean. Flames shot from the iron logs and their eyes flashed, though it was day. Thus did the iron monsters hail the deed of Hralekana.

Shortly afterward, all of them, except for the *Rainbow Whale*, turned and sailed toward the sun, now well above the horizon. We swam slowly on, thinking of how we might honor Hralekana.

We were carrying him back to the pod, the pod that now was traveling toward the krill and the summer feeding grounds. While

233

we swam, we spoke in low tones among ourselves. We decided the pod should carry Hralekana to his cavern far under the waves, or even better, to the Ice at the End of the World. There, under the ice shelf, in those cold blue waters, he would be preserved for later generations to honor. We and the other peoples of the sea would provide an eternal guard for him who saved the oceans, and maybe the whole globe, from so great a disaster.

It was with such thoughts that we tried to console each other as we swam that day. In the afternoon when I rose for air, the rubber raft pulled alongside of me, and Mark, his face several shades whiter, made sounds with his mouth little louder than a clam's. I couldn't understand what he wanted. The faint sounds continued until the picture flashed in my mind of his climbing onto Hralekana's back to be close to his friend one last time. I called to Aleea and Lewtë and they halted. The rubber boat pulled alongside Aleea, and Mark climbed onto her back and from hers to Hralekana's. The human choking noise began as he climbed and I saw water streaming down his face. Mark lay flat by Hralekana's blowhole, his flippers extended straight out on either side, and pressed his face into the hide of his old friend. He gave out a long, tapering moan that sounded almost like a Humpback's.

Aleea and Lewtë took up their positions and we carried the two along as the sun set among brilliant clouds, fiery, casting a light across the water. In that light Hralekana glowed as if on fire. Thus did the day in its dying salute the greatest of white whales.

Freely my tears came again as we carried him, and our keening and lamentation traveled far over the waves. Gone. He was gone, and we were desolate.

Mark continued to make the choking noises, his face pressed to Hralekana's skin, while I swam alongside, keeping watch over him.

Suddenly he raised his head and stared; he looked as if he'd seen a shark. I glanced around, but saw nothing. Mark pressed his head again to Hralekana's back, lifted and shook it, and stared at me, baffled.

I swam closer.

He pointed to his ear. "Did you hear it?"

I didn't know what he meant.

"A thump," he explained, pointing to his ear and to Hralekana. He pressed his head down again.

I called to Aleea and Lewtë.

Mark pressed his flipper to his lips and made a hissing noise, "Shh!" He kept his head down by the blowhole a long time, eyes wide open.

Minutes later he jerked his head up: "There it is again."

All three Humpbacks now pressed our ears to Hralekana, listening.

We heard nothing. Minutes passed.

"This is foolish," I thought. "Grief has turned our brains."

Just then I heard it—a soft thump, a very soft thump. Easy to miss—or imagine?—from somewhere deep inside Hralekana. More minutes dragged by and I heard a second thump. And not long after that, a third.

None spoke. We hardly dared breathe. Was this some cruel joke? Simply air moving about in the body?

While I pressed hard against his side, something sticky moved over my skin. I backed off and saw a little blood trickling from one of his scratches—from more than one. The blood was cold, but it was moving. And then, I don't know if it was a trick of the dusk and the sun setting in the west, but the battered skin of Hralekana glowed whiter than before.

Next, as if from the depths of the sea, a whisper came. A shiver passed through me and I looked around to see if a wind had sprung up. The surface was still, reflecting the clouds. The whisper grew and a groan came from all around us in the water. The stiff flippers sticking out from Hralekana trembled and twitched, and his flukes moved, however slightly.

I blinked and looked again. His eye was open.

Chapter Twenty-One

While my vision swam and all was going dark, I felt myself pressed into the battered white hulk rising from the Black Deep. It was my own flesh, I knew, and even as consciousness failed and the dark rushed in, I felt cramped and many pains shot through me. I fled from these into blessed unconsciousness.

The next thing I knew, I heard a faint sound. It was dark and I couldn't say where I was. I tried to move flippers and flukes but I couldn't feel them. The sound grew clearer—a choking sound. My heart leaped as I recognized Mark's weeping. He was close by.

I tried moving flippers and flukes again and felt only a tingly numbness. They were there, but I could barely move them. I felt no pain, however. I tried opening one eye: nothing but darkness. Then, as if from the bottom of the sea, I saw a gray light growing brighter.

I felt my mind rise up from the half-conscious darkness and strength move in a strong tide from my heart to the ends of my flippers. I closed my eyes and opened them again onto a sea flooded pink by the setting sun. I felt the air go out and come in my blowhole, sweet as I've ever breathed, and I groaned from sheer pleasure.

I tried out flippers and flukes, striking the water. At that I heard four cries, whether of fear or surprise it was hard to tell. I felt two warm, familiar bodies press against mine—Aleea and Lewtë on each side wailing and shedding tears. Hrūna suddenly appeared in front of me, choking on his speech, drops of oil streaming from his eyes.

On top of me I felt a small weight—Mark—his face wet as he tried to speak.

My own tears came and I laughed a long laugh from sheer joy, at being in the midst of those I loved, without pain, whole in all my parts, under a fair sky in warm waters.

I heard a familiar *thrug thrug* as the *Rainbow Whale* pulled alongside, bright in the setting sun, her rail lined with crew cheering and climbing overboard.

Through their tears the others were trying to speak. Mark finally controlled himself long enough to ask, his voice shaking, "You are alive?"

"Yes," I said, and now the mystery of all that had been revealed to me was clear, from my vision at the Springs of Fire in the other ocean through all my Seeings since, including those on my journey to the Kraken and while my body floated unconscious. "Do you think I could die that easily?"

In reply, I felt Mark's flippers dig in as he pressed himself to me. Aleea and Lewtë moved closer on either side, while Hrūna in his joy rolled against me from below. Their glad cries mingled with my own. Never had the crew of the *Rainbow Whale* heard a stranger collection of sounds from a pod of whales. Sweet and low were the words exchanged among us five that night and over the following day.

A full moon rose in the east while the sun was setting the next day. Dusk climbed from the water, the round disk of the moon brightened to silver, and the *Rainbow Whale* circled us while we swam slowly toward the Pole.

Through the water came a whisper, then a faint vibration, last a far-off babble of voices. The pod was headed our way. Somehow they'd received the news and young and old were hurrying to meet us. We swam faster.

The moon was not even halfway through her leap when silver geysers rose on the horizon where the pod breached to hail us. As they drew closer, fountain after fountain of foam flew up.

While they were still a good distance off, the spiraling white and black shapes of Hvala and Lūvah leaped in front of them, rising and falling in unison.

At last the twins swam straight toward us, squealing all the way. Glad was I to take each under a flipper and press them to me. They babbled so fast I couldn't understand what they were saying. Then the two darted away, swimming in a rapid circle around the five of us, leaping nimble as dolphins over us, drenching poor Mark on my back, who laughed in delight.

The rest of the pod arrived, three familiar pairs of wings circling them in the moonlight. As Ross landed on my back with a glad squawk, deep voices and high struck up a melody, for it was the night of a full moon. Suddenly the sea was alive with music as Humpbacks breached, leaped high, and dove deep. All of us joined in singing a gloria under the moon.

The moon breached across the sky while the pod sang to me and I sang back, gladly telling them of my last journey to the fiery trench, as well as all I could of my earlier sojourns and Seeings in the Deep. So beautiful was the night, I might have thought I'd passed into another world, if my scratches and blisters hadn't stung while they healed.

The deep voices of the males welled up from the bottom of the sea, overlaid by the intricate melody of the females and the high staccato notes of the calves at their play. All night Aleea and I lay pressed side to side, singing back and forth to each other while the twins leaped whistling in a bright circle about us, sending silver spray flashing to the moon.

Halfway through our singing, in the brief intervals of silence, we heard from a great distance the singing of the mermen and mermaids, and we sang more softly now, listening as their song blended with our own.

Meanwhile Mark lay on my back by my blowhole, and in the midst of that symphony of voices I heard his small human voice, weak and quavering, blend in as the gloria streamed up to the moon:

> The silver moon rises over a silver sea,
> Which gives the light back lithe on its waters,
> Giving glory to where glory has come from,
> As to the Lord of Light, the great Whale of the Waters,
> Invisible to all except in the Deep.
>
> We honor now Hralekana-kolua
> Who took fire in his mouth and returned it to fire
> Before it ate ocean and the earth rising from it,
> Who passed through the fire and was not eaten by it,
> Who went to the Deep and defeated the darkness
> And returned to us with fire living within.

At long last the White Cow of the Moon dove into the western sea and the stars in the Tailspray of the Leaping Whale faded out one by one in the brightening sky. The voices of the pod fell silent as we huddled on the surface and drifted off to sleep.

I watched the salmon-pink dawn streak the east, snuffed in the air sweet with brine, and thought of how hungry I was for herring and krill, and of the meal we'd have later when I woke. I closed my eyes, listening to the night murmur of the pod, to the deep breathing of Aleea, asleep beside me, and to the light, quick breath of Hvala and Lūvah, where they dreamed and stirred between us.